HOW TO IMPROVE ADULT EDUCATION IN YOUR CHURCH

JEROLD W. APPS

AUGSBURG PUBLISHING HOUSE
MINNEAPOLIS, MINNESOTA

HOW TO IMPROVE ADULT EDUCATION IN YOUR CHURCH

Copyright © 1972 Augsburg Publishing House

Library of Congress Catalog Card No. 72-78560

International Standard Book No. 0-8066-1226-6

MANUFACTURED IN THE UNITED STATES OF AMERICA

1737846

Contents

Introduction

The idea for this book came many years ago when I was a boy warming a hard pew in a little Lutheran Church in Central Wisconsin. Sunday morning was church time, except those Sundays when farm work took precedence or when a snowstorm blocked the country road, making travel impossible.

There was no Sunday school for the children in those days so youth and adults got the same treatment, Sunday after Sunday. Our pastor was a kindly man who stood ramrod straight and preached with a strong clear voice about heaven, hell, and why you should give more money to the church. Occasionally, a Sunday was devoted to what some missionary was doing in the bowels of Africa, but this usually turned into a "give money to the missions" session not unlike the regular money pleas of the church.

At 12, I started confirmation instruction to learn what the Lutheran Church was all about and I learned enough about Scripture and Luther's Small Catechism to become an official confirmed member of the church.

My early perception of the church was an institution with a series of things to memorize—liturgy, prayers, what the church stood for. For me the church had little relation to my everyday life. I grew up wondering why there was no apparent connection, and with no connection why were we spending Sunday morning there. I could think of better things to do on a Sunday morning.

What I searched for as a youth and still search for as an adult is meaning, not memorization. I wanted to find out who I was, how I related to the church, and how the church related to my life. I didn't want to be a church member in the image of what someone else thought I should be. I wanted to ask questions. Did my dog Fanny go to heaven when she was killed by a car? She lived with me since I could walk, so I wondered. And what about the neighbor kids I played with and later worked with during threshing bees, and silo filling—what were their chances for heaven? The pastor couldn't convince me because they didn't go to church they were bad, because they were my best and only friends.

My questions weren't answered. I not only asked few questions, I had little time to think of them . . . I was too busy memorizing what a good Lutheran should know. We were taught to be listeners, to be obedient. We weren't taught to question, to seek meanings, to search for relationships.

Thus, the reason for this book. It's my opinion that a great many adults attending church today had similar experiences in their early church exposure. Many of these adults are still searching for meaning, a sense of what the church is about. The traditional worship services aren't giving them the answers.

"Modern man has been taught to question, to prove, to weigh pieces of evidence rationally; a church that insists he accept certain tales and certain ideas without question or argument cannot hold his respect." [1]

Youth and young adults are also questioning. They're taught to question, to seek answers, to search for relationships in their formal education. Yet today in our traditional church approaches, we aren't answering young people's questions. We aren't providing an opportunity for young adults to relate their religion to their world. As a result we're losing young people. They're dropping out of church. They tell us the church is no longer relevant to their lives. And we answer them by saying, "You'll come back when you get a little older—the church will look better to you when you're more mature."

Some young people will come back. But I argue that many won't. We have lost them by not listening to their pleas for meaning in the church, by not answering their questions about religion and its relationship to their lives.

Changes must be made if the church is to survive. One change that churches can make to help questioning adults and young people find answers is through a comprehensive adult education program. Obviously, other changes are necessary too, such as liturgical changes, innovative changes in worship, less emphasis on buildings and more emphasis on programs, less emphasis on increasing congregational size and more emphasis on congregational involvement.

This book focuses on establishing an adult education program as a start toward modernizing the church. "The church has enormous membership and still enjoys a large measure of public respect, but it demonstrates, in most areas, only a fraction of its potential influence on our total culture. In countless communities the Christian cause seems unwilling to die and yet is unable to recover the secrets of true vitality." [2]

Material for the Book

As a professor of adult education at the University of Wisconsin, I became interested in my local church's adult education program several years ago. Throughout the book I'll refer to my personal experiences in planning and conducting church adult educational programs. I also believe that the field of adult education as practiced in the secular world has much to contribute to church adult education. Much of this book will be adaptions from the field of adult education, hopefully applied in a way that church people will find the information useful.

So there would be an array of opinions expressed by church people who are active in church adult education, I wrote to many pastors representing a variety of faiths. I asked these pastors three questions:

1. As you see it, what is the need for adult Christian education on contemporary problems?

2. Relate one example of an adult Christian education program conducted in your church including how the program was planned, methods used, resources obtained, etc.

3. What problems did you experience, for example, when dealing with controversial issues?

About 40 pastors answered my request. Much of what you'll read in this book will be real life experiences and thoughtful insights expressed by these pastors. My concern isn't to show what a particular denomination or church is doing, but to use what they are doing as examples of how a church can plan and carry out an adult education effort. No attempt is made to evaluate or comment on the "goodness" of a church's adult education activity. Only that church can determine the value of a particular program.

1

The Church and Adult Education

Before discussing approaches to adult education in the church, let me share some of my assumptions that form a foundation for this study. Although you might not agree with all the assumptions, I share them so you know my thinking and why I make certain proposals for adult education programs.

1. *I assume the church wants to change.* It's searching for ways of changing but often feels inadequate as to how and by which means it should change. It receives conflicting advice from its members. The young people want new worship forms, a progressive group of adults want social action opportunities, and often a solid majority isn't sure what changes they want. Yet I believe change is wanted.

2. *The church has responsibility for passing on tradition to its members, but it also has responsibility to get involved in the community.* Paul Johnson says the church:

> . . . is a disruptive influence in the lives of men, making war on complacency and pricking the individual and the corporate conscience. It is at the same time a light house on the hill, a haven of rest, a custodian of great truths to which disturbed mankind can come for rest and for assurance.[1]

I am not suggesting the church throw away all its traditions and alienate itself from vast numbers of people who expect tradition. I am suggesting that the church, where it is not doing it, add the second dimension—becoming involved with the world.

3. *The church, if it is to survive, must relate to the world.* Passing on tradition isn't enough, as important as that may be to some church members. Many young people and adults see the church as irrelevant to their lives. They see it as an expensive, tax-evading institution, filled with myths and grand stories of the life hereafter. These people want a church that is interested in this life, this world. They won't accept a church that only instructs them for salvation. They want a church that helps them meet the everyday problems of living, how to cope with family tensions, how to communicate with teenagers. They want a church that's concerned with the problems of society, drug abuse, civil rights, war, population control. These are problems the church can help solve.

4. *Adult education is one way to help the church relate to the real world of today.* Granted it isn't the only way, but it is an important one. Ramsay says, "We must study the world and ourselves in it or be ignorant of what it means fully to be Christian today." [2]

Much of what is called adult education in the church doesn't do this. The more traditional forms of church adult education have been concerned with passing on the traditions of the church and studying the Bible without reference to contemporary life. This form of adult education often ignores the problems of society or the individual problems of members. I believe the church has the responsibility of providing adults with information and insight that will help them with their individual problems and will help them understand better the problems of society and the contributions they can make to solving these problems.

I believe many local churches want to make their adult education efforts more relevant to the real world, but they fear the controversy that may be involved, they fear no one will be interested, they're concerned whether the church should work in "these areas," and they lack leadership to organize and implement meaningful adult education activity.

I asked pastors from throughout the country about the role of church adult education on contemporary problems. A Baptist said:

> If our churches had turned their attention to contemporary problems years ago we would not have many of the problems that we have today in turning their attention to these problems. We have become so self-centered in our teaching that it left no room for other problems. We have become so concerned with saving ourselves that we might end up losing ourselves and the world in the process.

From a Methodist:

> It has always taken mankind a period of time to allow his morality to catch up with his science and his sociology. The uniqueness of our situation is that there appears to be something distinctly climactic about our age. We have less time to catch up than any previous generation. To have spent the half-to three-quarter hour segment of time available weekly in most churches for adult Christian education discussing the route the children of Israel followed in leaving Egypt, may have been foolish a century ago— it may be *sinful* today.

11

A Presbyterian pastor speaks:

It is my own feeling that, educationally, the church has been relatively bankrupt and that in the fastest way possible we need to confront people with the realities of the world, the need for decision and the awareness that finally they are the ones in charge of their own educational process and that all learning has to do with one's personal self-understanding.

From a Unitarian:

Without exaggeration, one may say there is a crying need for an effective way to make such values as justice, love, compassion, truth, reverence, operative in our society. Most people have given up. They have for practical purposes accepted fully the competitive standards of the dog-eat-dog market place. There is no sentiment in business. People have blocked off their vocational activities securely from their private lives.

From a Catholic these words:

A great majority of practicing Christians still think of their religion mainly in terms of consolation and strength to face the "marginal situations" of life and to achieve happiness in the life to come. They do not realize the servant role of the Christian and the Christian community, their vocation to love "in deed and in truth" by trying to change society so as to make a full human life possible for all men. If Christians do not begin far more generally to carry out this aspect of their vocation, the Christian churches haven't much future, and a great potential force for peacemaking, in the full biblical sense of "peace" will remain a force for law-and-order keeping, or become more so. Many Catholics, especially the affluent blue-collar, non-reading ones, are increasingly resentful at the "changes" in the church, at new methods of teaching religion, because so few efforts have been made to help them understand what is going on. These people feel threatened in their religion too. I am convinced, and take every opportunity to say so, that the task of trying to reach these bewildered people and help them understand the servant role of the Christian should have top priority in our Christian education concerns.

Unless the churches begin to look and act more like the pilgrim and servant churches they are meant to be, more and more of the intelligent and sensitive young are going to leave them and never come back. We are wasting our time on children and adolescents unless the life-cycle of the churches and of their adult members begins to look more truly loving than it does at present.

5. *The church touches more adults in a week than any other institution, yet it does little with them.* Millions of adults are walking through church doors each Sunday morning, yet few are reached with experiences that affect their lives and the problems of society. The church is missing an adult opportunity greater than that of any other institution in our society.

But there's hope. Many laymen and pastors alike see this great potential for church adult education. One pastor told me:

> By and large, there is no other place in the community where people can discuss things in an objective sense, except as other organizations from time to time spurt with one thing or another. But the church has an educational dimension for adults as well as children and youth. The educational programs of the church should include contemporary problems on a whole range of matters, personal, social, religious, and I would even say political and economic. By and large the church is not doing any of this very much or very well.

2

Problems in Developing Church Adult Education Programs

It would be most naive of me to suggest that you blunder blindly into a full blown church adult education program without first considering some of the problems. It may appear perfectly obvious that an adult education program is needed in your church. After reading this book you should have some insight into how to get such an adult education program started. Yet there are some cautions to consider, some problem areas to be concerned with.

1. *Confused Priorities*

Does your local church know its purpose? Can you ask members what the church is doing and get more than a general answer like "a spiritual home for the members?"

Sometimes it's easier to observe the decisions made by the congregation and determine priorities than to ask the question. When the church budget is discussed, are the members more concerned about the physical plant, the church building itself, than the program of the church?

Is there more concern for recruiting new members than concern for the problems of people and the problems of society? Is the church more concerned about maintaining itself, building a larger and larger congregation, and income than it is concerned for programs? If so, then a contemporary adult education program will face stormy weather.

A Baptist pastor expressed his concern:

> The capacity to deal with contemporary concerns in adult education programs hinges on the desire of the church to make this one of its emphases. If the church is not committed to contemporary involvement, such classes or groups can be the battle scene where conflict over the church's role erupts. Worse than that, using contemporary phrasing in the title and publicity, the classes can be merely confirmations of the status quo.

The question of what role should the church play in relating to contemporary problems is a pertinent one. One pastor raised the issue this way:

> What is the specific content of the Christian message as it is addressed to contemporary social issues? How can what we do in Christian education be something distinctive in the wide array of the educational opportunities offered in the community at large? Does that question even need to appear for a church? Does education, which enlightens a person about the issues of the world in which they live, offer its own validity, whether that is for a church or not?

The problem a congregation has as it wrestles with priorities is no small one. Some congregations have given up looking at contemporary problems once they discovered the complexity of them. A minister of Christian Education wrote:

> We have for so long neglected contemporary problems (except for the usual picayune problems of

drinking, Sunday entertainment, etc.) that when we are confronted with these problems they are so large that we throw up our hands in horror at the enormity of the situation and then say that the church should not get involved.

2. *Avoidance of Controversy*

When I asked pastors to tell me the problem that most plagued them in their adult education programs, they answered, "controversy."

For many people the church is thought of as a place where everyone agrees with everyone else. Serious doubt is raised about "those people" who raise questions that challenge the majority feelings. "The tendency is to suppress conflict within a group. It seems that there is almost an ethic that values sterile order over creative conflict," a Methodist minister said.

The contemporary world is a diverse one with many diverse opinions on social problems. It would be unnatural if some of that same diversity were not found in the church, for the congregation should be a cross section of the community in which it is found. Doubt could be raised about those churches that do not have diverse points of view represented, for these churches do not represent their communities.

A Lutheran pastor was not concerned about diverse opinion.

> As Christians we do not need to agree on everything we do as a parish; but we must do many things because there are many needs. These many needs can only be met by a variety of approaches. The church must be open to all sorts of approaches and allow no doors to be closed simply because some people might say, "This is not my cup of tea."

Several pastors made the point that adult education on contemporary problems is indeed risk taking and must be so if any real learning is to take place.

Without doubt, failure to deal adequately with conflict in adult education programs can have dire consequences. If conflict is pushed aside and not allowed to be expressed, programs are often shallow and bland and if conflict is not handled to prevent people from "taking sides" against each other, other consequences will occur.

As I mentioned earlier, a great deal of good can come from dealing with controversy if it is done properly. A Lutheran pastor shares this case study:

> The most controversial program we have had so far has been a discussion of the book *Couples* by John Updike. Pietistic persons were unable to understand beforehand the reasons for including this book in the course. One man, for example, appeared at the meeting of the church council (the official governing board of the congregation) to protest the inclusion of this book in the course. The other members of the church council assured him of their similar feelings, but went on to point out the need for Christians to be aware of life in the 20th century and facing life as it is lived (and presented in this novel).
>
> On the day the discussion was held many people were on hand who in the past have not participated in the adult education program. Some of them were obviously antagonistic. Others were merely curious. When the laywoman who presented the topic finished, the president of our church council said, "I came this morning with reservations and questions, but I leave realizing the value of discussing such a book in the context of our Christian faith." Obviously the controversy was handled properly by selecting the right leadership. That is the key to handling controversy—*the leadership*.

This pastor has identified competent leadership when discussing controversial topics as being of prime importance. Well-trained leadership is essential.

3. *Dependency*

Many adults attending adult education classes for the first time do not feel they have anything to contribute. They look to the instructor for the answers, and they see their role as passive recipients of knowledge. They see the church as the final authority on all questions. A Catholic wrote: "Parents don't want to let go of the 'how-far-can-you-go-before-it's-a-mortal-sin' way of teaching morality, especially sexual morality; they want the church to reinforce their authority."

Many pastors and laymen who are in teaching roles feel they must speak the authoritative word for the church. A Methodist pastor said:

> I find it difficult for many Christian teachers to use the "I don't know" response. When one has to have all the answers, he has created an impossible task for himself. Undoubtedly, we are still caught up in a prepositional task which places much more emphasis on "to" than it does on "with." The former may be the result of paternalistic ways, authoritarian conditions, and psychologically "safe" methodology. The latter approach, "withness," calls for openness, flexibility, mutual search and discovery, and the desire for renewal.

4. *Communication Problems*

A subtle and often overlooked problem that can tear apart a church adult education program is a lack of communication among people. Establishing good communication is one principle the skilled discussion leader follows when dealing with controversial issues. Communication means talking back, questioning, searching for meaning.

A Wisconsin pastor comments:

> Very few run-of-the-mill adult groups are willing, or even able, to participate in a meaningful dialog without such strong emotional involvement which

usually precludes their ability to listen much less to hear what someone else is saying. Unless there has been some real training and learning in the area of the art of listening it is so easy to pass judgments and then feel obligated to continue that kind of rationale without ever really evaluating the alternatives available. Adult education today needs to help individuals see that there can be disagreement of mind and yet a continuation of openness and willingness to learn from the other person's point of view. Probably the greatest area of need in the adult world is the ability to communicate with one another. We have so many little games that we play where we carefully wear the proper masks and have adequate insulation to keep from revealing our true selves and the kind of person we really are. More and more is being written these days on "the art of listening." We can easily see the bamboo, wire, and stone walls of separation, but it is so difficult to see and to recognize the similar walls that are built up between individuals that keep us from really sharing with one another the real dreams of life.

5. Lack of Meaningful Study

A Massachusetts pastor states the problem: "Adult religious education has sunk into a morass of study-discussion on the assumption that to know the words and to have the right ideas is to have gotten an education."

Attending a Sunday morning adult education session with 50 or 60 other people assembled to hear a guest speaker is adult education, to many church members. It may be, but at a superficial level. At best this type of adult education programming provides only an awareness of some problem or concern to the participant. There is little opportunity for more in-depth learning to occur. This type of adult education activity will often draw large numbers, but numbers do not assure that quality education is occurring. It may mean the opposite, for people may see the Sunday morning large group experience as one type of entertainment.

6. *Inadequate Resources, Poorly Trained Pastors, and Lay Leaders*

As I meet and talk with pastors, I continue to be amazed at the number who say to me, "If only I had gotten some adult education instruction in my formal schooling." One pastor told me, "I would love to have traded several courses in Greek for just one in adult education."

And with pastors poorly trained in adult education it follows that lay leaders may have little preparation. The pattern is changing, but slowly. Several of the major Protestant denominations have active adult education units in their central offices. Some Catholic dioceses have made substantial progress in providing in-service opportunities for clerics with adult education responsibilities.

As was mentioned, poorly trained leadership can cause discussions of controversial issues to blow up. Improper leadership may never allow a group enough time to develop as a group. The untrained person is often intent on some kind of quick success with his group and thus never allows for in-depth probing of the issues.

There is also a problem of dependency on written materials from the central office. A Lutheran pastor comments:

> Too much of the contemporary printed materials are unsuccessful in dealing with needs in the area of adult Christian education because: (1) they are hurried, futile attempts to shut the floodgates of clamoring for relevant materials, (2) they are often too lengthy, (3) if course materials (textbooks), they require a commitment for a course of study for more than a six-week period, (4) they are written by persons who have never been required to be relevant to first-line contemporary problems in their own lives

(or who have failed when confronted), (5) there is a stereotyped image of Christian education generally which is not conducive to learning, (6) authors are too often "self-styled educators" or "pseudo-educators" (this unfortunately, includes graduates of university schools of education), (7) there is too much philosophizing and not enough of the "nitty gritty," (8) teachers' guides and other "helps" rarely emphasize the broad spectrum of understanding, or lack of it, that Christian adults have concerning what the church is all about (or what it should be about).

But why be dependent on central office materials when there are so many contemporary and current materials that can be used as resource materials for adult education programs? Why must church leadership feel so dependent on materials written by one overworked staff at headquarters, when there are thousands of interesting and useful resources all around?

3

The Adult Learner

When adult education is mentioned, many adults respond "Go to school again? I haven't been in a classroom since I was 18—you expect me to start again at my age?"

Why do adults respond this way when education is suggested? We need to know something about the adult as a learner before planning contemporary church adult education programs.

Adults are not children who have outgrown the school room desk. Thus, sometimes it may be difficult for an effective youth teacher to work with adults, without first gaining some basic understanding of adults as learners.

BASIC CHARACTERISTICS OF ADULT LEARNERS
Often Insecure in an Adult Education Setting

They are fearful of making a mistake, saying the incorrect thing, doing poorly, and having others think them incompetent. Adults feel they have a reputation to maintain. They don't want to be placed in an embarrassing situation or a situation where their lack of knowledge will become evident. This characteristic is especially true of adults who participate or who are potential participants in church education classes.

Adults who are becoming acquainted with religious education often feel embarrassed. If asked to read from the Bible, adults are fearful there will be words they cannot pronounce. They fear not finding the correct place in the Bible as quickly as others if asked to turn to a particular passage. This is why adults often stay home from church adult education and tell you, "We're interested, but we just don't have time." Their real reasons for not attending are often quite different from the reasons they give.

Concern for Solving Life's Problems

Adults participate in adult education activities to find solutions to their problems and meet their needs. In a study of participation patterns, Houle,[1] an adult education researcher, learned that adults participate in educational activities for three basic reasons. First, some attend because they have a specific problem to be solved. For example, some adults are concerned how they as individuals can contribute to solving a particular social problem that exists in their community.

Second, some attend because they like to learn; they have become accustomed to acquiring new ideas and they like it. Participating in religious educational activities is another opportunity for them to satisfy their craving for new knowledge and insight.

And finally, a third group of adults participates in adult education activities to get away from home for an evening, to meet and to be with other people. What is taught is only incidental to their attendance and participation.

Of course, some participate for a combination of reasons, in some instances all three of the above reasons.

What are some adult needs? Robert J. Havighurst has researched adult needs and has divided the adult years into three groups: "early adulthood," "middle age," and "later maturity." Havighurst suggests there are 10 social roles for these three groupings—mate, worker, parent, homemaker, son or daughter of aging parents, citizen, friend, religious affiliate, organization member, and user of leisure time. As an adult moves through the three phases of adult life, the requirements for performing each of the social roles changes.[2]

These are the needs that motivate adults to participate in adult education activities. The needs of each age group varies, indeed there is much variation within each age group. As we plan adult education activities, it's important to realize that needs are real to adults and that they are developmental. For example, the need to find and get started in an occupation precedes the developing of leisure time activities.

Obviously religious adult education won't provide learning opportunities for all of the adult needs as expressed by Havighurst. Yet many of the needs may be met through thoughtful programming.

Variety of Experiences and Education

A class of children is generally made up of youngsters of similar ages with quite similar background experiences. They have all grown up during the same period of time, and have all had a similar formal educational experience. But a group of adults will vary considerably, not only in age, which means they will have grown up during different periods, but also in amount of formal education.

Think of Time Differently than Do Children

Young people think of education as preparing for the future. Not so with most adults. Adults are looking for solutions to needs and problems they are now experiencing. The idea that "education is good for you" may occasionally work with young people (there is doubt here too), but it seldom works when the adult learner is considered. The adult wants to know why and how a particular adult education experience will be useful to him. And for most adults useful means right now, not 5 or 10 years from now.

Some Believe Age Prevents Learning

There are still people who feel education is for children and that adults cannot or no longer need to learn. E. L. Thorndike, a psychologist, studied the learning abilities of adults from 14 to 50 years old. The results of his research were published in 1928 and in summary say:

a. The best time for learning is between 20 and 25 years of age.

b. From age 25 to about age 42 there is a decline in capacity for learning of approximately one percent per year.[3]

Other researchers following Thorndike were more optimistic in their reports of adults' learning capabilities. Irving Lorge, followed up Thorndike's adult learning research and concluded that the intellectual power of the adult does not change from age 20-60.[4]

But the rate or speed of learning, because of natural aging processes[5] decreases as age progresses. Eyesight reaches its maximum at about age 18 and steadily declines until age 40. From age 40 to 55, the ability to see declines sharply.

The same trend is true for hearing ability. Maximum hearing ability occurs between ages 10 and 15. After age

15, there is a steady decline to age 65. Older adults also hear more slowly. Even without hearing loss, an older person will have difficulty understanding someone who speaks rapidly.

Rate of learning is thus affected by these natural slowing down processes, and actual losses in hearing and seeing abilities. Along with these physiological changes, there is also an increased fear of failing as adults get older.

Because Thorndike's research included rate of performance as one of the criteria for measuring ability to learn, his findings were more pessimistic than Lorge and others who followed Thorndike. Most researchers now agree that ability to learn is not adversely affected by age, indeed in many instances the experience older people have is an asset to learning. But we must remember, learning speed slows down with age.

Adults must be constantly reminded that they can learn, that adults are learning, and there are no reasons why they cannot continue to learn throughout their lives.

Young Adults Bring New Perspectives

Adult education programmers, in the church and elsewhere, often overlook the new perspective young adults bring to educational programs. Young adults, who are already in our programs, will come in increasing numbers—if we are willing to make adjustments in our programs to recognize their differing needs.

Many of today's youth question the approaches used in the public schools and in the colleges and universities. These young people will also question meaningless and unimportant religious adult education, and we must be ready to cope with their questions.

I don't think we can assume, as many people seem to, that young people, once they reach age 21 will act like the middle-age adults we now have in our programs.

True, some of them will. But many will come to our programs with a value system that is quite different from their parents and other older adults. What are some of the value differences?

Many young people are choosing personal rights over property rights, human needs over technological requirements, cooperation over competition, sexuality over violence, consumer over producer, ends over means, openness over secrecy, personal expression over social reforms, distribution over concentration.[6]

Many of today's youth see adults as provincial in their interests, materialistic, resistant to change, compromising with their values, overly concerned with security, disinterested in other people's problems, overly respectful of people in authority, and inconsistent in what they practice and what they preach. These young adults see the world differently, want more participation in decisions that affect them, are more tolerant of other people's peculiarities, want more freedom to do what interests them as long as it doesn't harm anybody.

Young people approach problems from a broader perspective than former generations. And feelings and emotions are an important part of their decision making. These young adults place more emphasis on the human side of problems than any former generation.

Those of us associated with church adult education must realize that the young adults who will seek out our programs aren't the same as the older adults whom we've comfortably worked with for many years. These young adults will demand that we consider their often differing value system when they participate in adult education—and if we aren't ready to change, we'll be passed by.

4

Important Adult Education Basics

Some adults are apprehensive about church adult education because they don't know what it is. Maybe it's the word education. Unfortunately many adults had unpleasant formal education experiences and developed undesirable attitudes toward education.

We're challenged to help potential participants in our adult education programs see education differently than they remembered it as youngsters in an elementary or secondary school. And we're also challenged to make certain our adult education programs aren't like those remembered.

Many people responsible for adult education programs often, and sometimes unconsciously, follow the same educational patterns they observed when they were students.

Before organizing a contemporary church adult education program a basic question must be answered: What is the purpose?

PURPOSE OF ADULT EDUCATION

What is the ultimate objective of our adult education efforts? What are we trying to achieve? I believe many who work in church adult education are confused about what they're trying to accomplish. Often, I believe, church adult education goals are too narrow. Perhaps we've followed too closely the dictionary definition of learning: "Knowledge or skill acquired by instruction or study."

For too many people, educators and learners alike, learning is thought of as acquiring units of information—the amount of learning is related to the number of years you've spent in school, the number of college credits you've taken, or the number of Bible classes you've attended.

Too often I believe learning is thought of as acquiring precise knowledge, void of any emotion or sentimentality. It's thought of as replication rather than interpretation, memorization rather than integration.

As a result of this narrow learning orientation, little time is spent by those responsible for church adult education considering ultimate meaning, subjectivity and personal feelings, speculation about causes, influences, and relationships that defy quantification.

Many adults, particularly those middle-aged or older, come to our programs having experienced a formal education program that often had a narrow view of learning.

These adults have been dehumanized by I. Q. scores, personality rating scales, and class-ranking procedures. They're products of an educational system that classified them as A students or D students, as achievers or under-achievers, or as dropouts. The wholeness of their self—their total personality—was reduced to a symbol suggesting average, superior, or mediocre. Thus, many adults coming to our programs are products of a system that ranked them, rated them, graded them, and taught them to all think alike.

It's essential then, that we change our image of what adult learning should accomplish. I believe the purpose of contemporary church adult education is to free people to be themselves, to be individuals, to develop their own potentials. John Gardner, in his book *No Easy Victories,* says:

> All education worthy of the name enhances the individual. It heightens awareness, or deepens understanding, or enlarges one's powers, or introduces one to new modes of appreciation and enjoyment. It promotes individual fulfillment. It is a means of self-discovery.[1]

Our aim for contemporary church adult education must not separate facts from emotion. We must deal with the whole man—his needs, his loves, his hates, his prejudices. No longer can we accept memorization of isolated facts as an appropriate aim for adult education efforts. The aim must be broader.

Adult education in the church must be real, must touch people "where they live," relate to their lives as they live them. Adult education must be seen as one of the most important things a person does in his life, not as a frill that uses up time when there is nothing else that demands attention.

POOR IMAGE

Unfortunately, many people think of adult education as activities that nudge the fringes of people's lives. Cake decorating, fly tying, golf lessons, and a host of other recreational activities encompass adult education for many.

Recreational activities for adults are important, and adult education programs can help to further develop recreational skills. But this is only one small part of what an adult education program can be.

Yet, to many, adult education means recreational activities and nothing more. People with this attitude toward adult education must be helped to see there is more. Indeed, the potential is unlimited for adult education programming in the church.

Another image some people have of adult education, whether conducted in the church or outside, is method. We hear people, when adult education is mentioned, say, "Oh, you mean getting people in small groups to discuss something," or "You mean a retreat to discuss something," or "You mean a conference where people get together to hear somebody talk."

Again to some, the method used—the means of doing adult education—has become the end. How often have you heard an adult education planning committee start by saying, "We're scheduled to have this weekend retreat—now what are we going to do? How will we organize it, whom will we invite?"

This kind of planning is like building a house and talking about what kind of paneling to use on the walls when you should be asking whether you should be building a house at all. Perhaps the particular housing needs could be better met by putting up tents, or maybe constructing an apartment building.

Many adult education programmers have brought this image of adult education and method as synonymous on themselves. In their haste to design programs, they've chosen the approach or method they'll use before asking the basic questions:

1. What are we trying to accomplish?

2. With whom are we trying to accomplish it?

Not until these questions are answered should method be considered.

Adult Learning

What happens when an adult participates in a religious education program? Hopefully, there is change. Basically, that's what education is—change. Generally we think of change in three areas: (1) change in knowledge —adults knowing something after the class they did not know before, (2) a change in skill—adult students being able to do something after participating in the class that they couldn't do before, and (3) a change in attitude— thinking and feeling differently about something after participating in the class.

One, two, or all three of these changes might occur depending on the subject matter of the program. For example, if a group of adults discusses, in a series of sessions, the changing role of the American family you might expect a learning outcome to be greater knowledge of the forces in society that affect the modern day American family (one possible knowledge change). Another outcome might be changed attitudes about the role of the American family—that the participants in these sessions might think and feel differently about the family role as a result of attending the sessions (a possible attitude change).

Of course, there'll be additional outcomes from the sessions: the group members will get to know each other and will come to enjoy each other's company; they may tell others about the group and the number participating in the sessions may increase; they perhaps will leave the sessions with a feeling of well being for having taken part.

These are all outcomes from the adult education sessions. Although these additional results are important and often necessary for successful programs, we must continue to focus on the basic outcomes—changes in knowledge, skill, and attitudes.

If we can agree on the essential basic outcomes of

adult education efforts, what can we do to help ensure that learning (a change in the adults who attend our sessions) takes place?

Providing an opportunity for learning isn't an easy task—there's no set of "first we do this" and "then we do that" steps to follow. However, there are some guidelines to consider. The logic is this—if we provide these guidelines, then it's more likely that learning will take place.

GUIDELINES FOR ADULT LEARNING

Focus of Learning Must Be on the Individual

Learning is a very personal thing; only the learner can do it. The focus of learning can't be on the group leader for he's only one of many resources to the learner; the focus can't be on the subject matter or the learning materials used either . . . it must be on the potential learner.

Because of the magnificent uniqueness of every person, what is heard, seen, smelled, felt is different for everyone. Experience is perceived through the senses. And because each person perceives the identical object or experience in a unique way and because each person has a different background of experience to relate the new perception, the learning that takes place in each person will be different.

This guideline is violated more often than any other in adult education. Too often the focus is on the group. We hear adult educators say, "And what are the needs of the retired people?" or "What are the needs of young married groups in our church?"

We must start by asking, "What are the needs of this person, that person, and the one sitting over there?" Once we have thought about individuals' needs, then we can look for common problems or needs and use this as a basis for organizing a learning group.

No one can learn for anyone else. When we try to impose our ideas on someone else under the guise of teaching, little learning takes place. The individual must discover for himself the meaning of the ideas. And he'll discover the meaning of ideas as they relate to his problems and needs. We can't solve problems for people, we can only provide opportunities and ideas that will allow the individual to solve his own problems.

If the ideas and opportunities offered don't relate to individual problems and needs, then little learning can be expected.

Focus Must Be on the Whole Person

We must be willing to deal with both the emotional and the intellectual aspects of learning at the same time. We must be willing to consider the emotions, feelings, hates, and loves individuals have at the same time that we deal with ideas and facts.

This isn't easy. Education has often purposely avoided dealing with the entire person. Neat packages of facts to be memorized by persons with no attention to the emotions or feelings that are present in the group has been emphasized.

No learning results when the entire person isn't considered. On occasion, negative learning may take place. For example, if a small group of adults discussing racial prejudice disagree among themselves, the disagreement must be dealt with. Presenting facts without facing the issue of the disagreement may lead people to leave the session with feelings of hostility toward each other (negative learning) and few if any facts or ideas about racial prejudice will be learned. I'll discuss later how to deal with disagreement in a learning situation to provide positive outcomes.

Occasionally, when learning is focused on the whole person that learning may be unpleasant to the person.

It's not easy for a person to give up old ways of thinking about something and change. It's not easy for a person to discover that something he had thought for years was fact is untrue.

And it's not easy for a person to be open and free to express his inner thoughts about himself in relation to what's being discussed. Though at times it may be painful to the person, it's in unpleasant situations that real learning takes place. The result isn't a shallow learning with memorization of unrelated facts. When the whole person is involved in the learning process, the person is most apt to change. And change, as we mentioned earlier, is what learning is all about.

1737846

The Learner Must Be Actively Involved

There are three types of involvement I'd like to mention: (1) making decisions about what's to be learned, (2) involvement in the learning process itself, and (3) making decisions about whether or not learning took place.

Some educators argue that making decisions about what is to be learned, determining whether learning took place, and how the process could be improved are all a part of the learning process. Basically I agree with that position, but I separate the three types of involvement mainly to discuss them.

Making Decisions About What Is to Be Learned. How often have we said, "Here's what I think this group will be interested in doing" without ever finding out if what *you* think they're interested in is what *they* are interested in. This is violated often in our adult education efforts as we are able to get many kinds of packaged programs that can be quickly utilized.

For learning to be important and significant, people must have an opportunity to express what they want to learn. I don't mean the learner has all the responsibility for finding the content, the ideas, the facts that he'll be learning. He doesn't have the responsibility for finding the resource materials that he'll use, although he may have some involvement here too.

Making decisions about what's to be learned is to find out from the learner something about his interests, his problems, his needs. This information is then used as a basis for organizing learning experiences for the person.

There are many ways to involve the learner in making decisions about what's to be learned. You can ask him, with a check sheet, what his interests are. You can have a group of people meet together to discuss what they'd like to learn. You can talk to people informally, when and where you meet them and discover something about their learning interests. It isn't so important what involvement approach you use—but that persons be involved.

When people feel what they're learning is what they want to learn, then it's more likely that learning will occur.

Involvement in the Learning Process Itself. This involvement is another way of saying learning by doing. Learning is most efficient in an atmosphere where the learner is actively involved in the process. Often though, the instructor or group leader is active and the group members sit passively by watching and listening. The reverse would provide a better atmosphere for learning— the learners actively pursuing questions with each other and with the leader while the leader plays a contributing but not a dominating role.

For member involvement in the learning process, a climate of trust between the learners and the group leader and among the learners themselves must be developed. Learners must feel free and open enough to discuss issues with each other. And likewise, there must be a feeling of trust between the learners and the instructor.

The group leader or instructor must be willing to accept many alternative answers to a problem. He must not be of the mind that there are single answers to questions, that he as the group leader has them, and that it's his responsibility to transfer these ideas from his head to the heads of the learners. Nothing squelchs learning involvement faster than the "my head to your head" philosophy of learning.

Later I'll discuss a variety of techniques that can be used to insure member involvement in the learning process.

Determining What Learning Took Place. It follows that if learners are given the opportunity to determine what they'll learn and are involved actively in the learning process itself, then they should have an opportunity to determine if their learning goals were reached.

If the learning is individualized, then the learner can determine best the extent change has taken place—that learning has occurred. The group leader can help the learner in this evaluation. He can give his impressions of the changes that have occurred in the person and he can indicate where further change might occur. But the evaluation of learning is the responsibility of the learner himself. The role of the leader is to help the learner complete the process, not to do it for him. The leader evaluating the learner violates the "individual determining what will be taught" philosophy. If someone else, such as the leader, evaluates the learning, the leader's criteria may or may not be the same criteria the learner would have used himself.

The Leader Must Be Willing to Take Risks

When the learner is free to make decisions about what's learned and is actively involved in the learning process as a participant, there is risk. The learner will make mistakes, there'll be failures. The leader must be willing to take these risks. Indeed, this kind of risk taking often turns an otherwise bland learning situation where everyone knows the end product will be successful into something that is dynamic and more lifelike. Living is a constant risk . . . there's always the possibility of failure. And likewise, learning experiences should also have risk. Mistakes shouldn't be seen as catastrophes, but as opportunities.

When there's freedom for the learner to make mistakes, he has many more options open to him and his learning can be more creative. If the learner can choose only those options or approaches that have previously succeeded, the excitement of learning evaporates, and many never before tried approaches continue to be never tried.

Adult educators must learn to accept errors as an integral part of learning as they are of living, and that a learning situation isn't always designed so all the answers are "right" and that mistakes are never made.

Learner Seen as an Idea Source

In an adult learning situation there are many potential sources of ideas. Often overlooked is the learner himself. Because of their many years of experience, of problem solving and learning, adults have much to contribute to most questions discussed by a learning group.

The leader, though, often sees himself as the sole knowledge source, perhaps along with a book that he uses, and seldom thinks of the wealth of knowledge represented in the learners themselves.

When learners feel that they're free to participate in the learning situation, and when they feel trust exists, then they're most apt to share their experiences. Adult education leaders should strive for this type of sharing atmosphere.

The leader should see himself as one source of ideas

to the learner, but the leader should help the learner see that he, too, is an idea source—a very important one.

Often with new groups of adults, it's difficult to get adults to freely contribute. They feel that they've come to the learning situation to "get the answers" and the leader has them.

It's understandable that many adults feel this way. Many of them are products of a formal school system where the instructor and the textbook were the sources of ideas and the learner was a passive recipient.

But in an adult education setting, we must work to change this attitude and help adults recognize that they have much to contribute in solving their own problems and needs and helping others to solve their problems and needs. Active involvement in determining what's to be learned and active involvement in the learning process are steps toward helping the learner recognize the potential source of ideas he has.

The ideal toward which the leader should work is a learning situation where there's complete sharing of ideas with a variety of sources for these ideas. The leader is one source, the learners another source, outside resource people, films, tapes, books, and so on are also sources.

The process of education is gleaning ideas from these various sources to help solve the problems and needs people have. Thus, the focus for the learning must always first be on the person not on the ideas. We must continually remind ourselves that learning is a change in people, and this change isn't only the acquisition of a variety of ideas from outside sources, but is a discovery of ideas within the person himself which will help him to change.

Confrontation Is Permitted

If we accept the philosophy that there's no right or wrong answer to many problems but a variety of opinions, then we must be willing to deal with differences of opinion that will develop in learning groups.

Some leaders are quite fearful of confrontation and feel that learning groups should be happy, congenial groups of people where there's never a difference of opinion. If people are encouraged to be free and to express their ideas about problems, there'll be differences of opinion and there'll be confrontations. The learning atmosphere must be able to accept differing opinions. The idea that for every problem there must be a right and a wrong answer must be abolished. For active learning to take place there must be room for many ideas, some of which will be in direct opposition to each other.

Later I'll discuss how to deal with confrontation and disagreement in a learning group.

The Process of Learning Is as Important as the Content of Learning

So far we've said that helping people to solve their problems and meet their needs is an appropriate goal for learning. We don't want to lose sight of this purpose. But there's another purpose to be achieved in a learning situation.

How the learning takes place, or the process of learning, isn't often perceived directly by the learners. This is understandable. The learner is busy working with ideas and problems and doesn't focus any attention on the procedures and techniques the leader uses to help him seek ideas and reach solutions.

One goal for learning should be to help people become self-directed, independent learners. We should strive for learners who by themselves can deal with ideas, seek out idea sources, and make decisions about which ideas contribute to solving their problems.

Thus, one goal we should work toward is helping learners learn the process of learning, helping learners recognize which approaches to learning work best for them, helping learners become comfortable with problem solving approaches, helping learners identify their problems and needs, helping learners evaluate solutions to their problems so they can select the one solution which best fits them.

This is a longtime goal that isn't accomplished in one or two sessions. But we must keep it in mind so learners don't develop a dependence on some leader or instructor to always lead them through learning situations.

These learning guidelines are helpful to me as I plan and work with adult groups. You may not agree with all of them, you may wish to add to the list or subtract from it. I hope you'll use the list as a starting place in thinking about planning and conducting learning experiences for adults in your church. What's most useful is a list you develop, a list that comes from within you based on your background and experience, and the various ideas you've gleaned from this book and other sources.

Basic to all of this, is having some set of guidelines for your adult education operation. I believe everyone needs to have some kind of foundation for making decisions about his adult education program.

5

Developing Adult Education Objectives

PLANNING FOR ADULT EDUCATION

Planning for adult education isn't easy. And to many it's not the most exciting part of adult education programming. Most adult education leaders are action people. They want to be leading, to be teaching. They often see planning as something academic, something someone else ought to do.

But when someone else does the planning there can be problems. Many pastors and lay leaders responsible for adult education programming are anxious to use what someone else develops. They constantly ask their national offices to produce more courses, more materials that can be used in their programming.

Local church people are busy and often overloaded with many tasks in addition to their responsibilities for adult education. But not every program developed outside your local church will fit your church. Modification is often necessary. When courses and materials are rather arbitrarily adopted there's no continuity in a church's adult education programming. There's no long-term plan. Adult education becomes a disjointed collection of offerings depending on what's available from headquarters at a particular time.

A more sensible approach for adult education leaders to follow is to plan their own programs, using the resources available from the national offices when they're applicable.

I suggest four basic phases in adult education programming:

1. Determining the objectives for the adult education program.
2. Selecting learning approaches to meet the objectives.
3. Selecting learning experiences and methods.
4. Evaluating the program.

This chapter will focus on phase one, determining objectives for the adult education program. Succeeding chapters will focus on phases two through four.

DETERMINING OBJECTIVES

What is the adult education program to accomplish? This is the first question to answer in planning. But if your local church hasn't looked at its total program and made decisions about purpose, then this must be done before adult education objectives can be determined. Earlier I mentioned that many local churches are often confused about purposes and priorities. If that confusion is allowed to prevail, the adult education program will also be confused. Before an adult education program can be effective, there must be some overall direction established for the church wishing to conduct adult education.

A Case Example

Let me share with you an example of how Midvale Community Lutheran Church in Madison, Wisconsin, determined its goals and priorities, and how these goals became a basis for adult education planning.

The long-range planning effort started at the insistence of several lay church leaders who were concerned that Midvale was drifting and didn't know what it was trying to accomplish. There were also factions developing within the church, some feeling the church should become actively involved in one kind of activity, others opposing that activity but suggesting active involvement in something else.

Midvale has a church council of 12 members. Everyone except the president serves as chairman of a church committee of from 5 to 25 members

The church council discussed the problem of goals and direction at a regular meeting and decided to conduct a day and a half retreat for council members and committee members at a conference site away from Madison. A committee of three council members and the senior pastor planned the tentative retreat schedule.

Dr. William Streng from Wartburg Theological Seminary, Dubuque, Iowa, was invited to serve as resource person for the retreat. Before the retreat, participants were invited to read Chapter 1 of *Renewing the Congregation* by Robert W. Long and William Streng's book *In Search of Ultimates*.

The small group discussions on the first evening of the retreat were led by council members, and focused on the first chapter of *Renewing the Congregation*. Discussion group 1 considered "The Church and the World," group 2, "The Church and its Members," and group 3, "The Church and Worship."

The planning committee and the senior pastor prepared several questions and statements as discussion starters for each group.

THE CHURCH AND THE WORLD.

1. The world provides the agenda for the church.

2. Where is the church on Monday morning?

3. What is difference between God—Church—World, and God—World—Church?

4. Many parish congregations are popular because they're irrelevant to contemporary problems, they are a sanctuary from the problems of the world.

THE CHURCH AND ITS MEMBERS.

1. Is it true that the church
   —is overorganized?
   —should only serve its members?
   —should give first priority to its members?
   —should strive to preserve its tradition?

2. The church must be concerned with developing and maintaining the faith of its members and at the same time be concerned with the larger community and the world?

THE CHURCH AND WORSHIP.

1. Why worship?

2. Are worship forms important?

3. Is worship something that only can be done in a church building?

4. Should parents force a 15-year-old to go to church?

5. What are some guidelines for a worship form?

Reporters for each discussion section prepared written reports of what happened in their section.

The "Church and the World" group reported:

1. We must include "community" as well as the entire world in church programming.

2. New ideas are needed to accomplish "missionary" work in the world.

3. There's an information gap of the older generation explaining to the youth the meaning of traditional ways, and youth telling older people their views.

4. Should we take action as a church or action as an individual?

5. Cell groups could accomplish something in some controversial areas where the whole church couldn't act.

The "Church and Its Members" group reported:

1. The commitment that people have for our church is important. Have members sign a commitment to participate in church activities—perhaps each year each one signs a recommitment.
2. Education programs should be issue oriented.
3. We need to consider a more adequate use of our church building—should more than one religion use a church building?
4. Additional youth education offerings should be available beyond Sunday morning—youth should be invited to bring their friends?
5. Youth should have more opportunity to use the youth room.
6. We should devise ways of having more members participate in church activities—also in attending Sunday services and Communion.

The "Church and Worship" group reported:

1. Christians should become interested in Christian history to make religion more meaningful.
2. We shouldn't let forms get in the way of worship.
3. The liturgy should be brought up to date.
4. People have to get involved to make worship meaningful.
5. Tradition and unity are important aspects of worship.
6. Music is important to worship.
7. The efficiency of the sermon as an educational tool is questioned.
8. Could there be dialogue rather than sermon?

Following the opportunity to hear and interact with Dr. Streng, the larger group again broke into small discussion groups to consider program and priorities for Midvale. The four groups were "Education," "Evangelism and Fellowship," "Community Involvement," and "Worship."

The "Education" group reported:

1. The character of adult education has changed from social to study groups. We must make more effort to organize small discussion groups.
2. We must study our entire youth education program, inviting in outside consultants to help assess where we are now in our programming and where we need to go.
3. We must improve our teacher recruitment procedure and training program.

The "Evangelism and Fellowship" group reported:

1. We should develop new terms for evangelism and fellowship, because many people have negative impressions of these words.
2. Our evangelism program must focus on true concern for others.
3. Do we need more members at Midvale? Much of our concern should be with our present members who aren't involved.

The "Community Involvement" group reported:

1. We should train groups of people for certain aspects of church involvement.
2. People should commit themselves on what they'd like to do for the church and the community.
3. A bulletin board should be available with church and community activities listed so people are aware of help needed. People should sign up and then a person should be in charge of seeing that things are carried out.
4. A suggestion box should be available.
5. A "mothers for peace" group in our church should be started.

6. We should determine a procedure for priorities on how Midvale dollars should be spent.

The "Worship Group" reported:

1. Worship should be seen as a means to an end . . . not the end.
2. We believe the purpose of worship is to help people love one another.
3. There should be continued innovation in worship forms, with the congregation prepared for the changes to help ensure acceptance.
4. Task forces should be organized, in Sunday school, confirmation classes, youth groups, and adult groups, to prepare new forms of worship. Possible approaches could be through music, contemporary records, movie and photography groups, drama, writing, and such helps as rewriting present worship materials. Intensive work in these task forces would result in more education than a routine classroom, and results would enrich the entire congregation.
5. There should be alternative forms of worship offered, entirely new forms for those who desire it, the more traditional forms for those most comfortable with what they already know.

Council Discusses Objectives. The church council, following the retreat, discussed the next steps in its long-range planning effort and its search for goals and purpose.

At the next council meeting, a university professor of business management who is a member of Midvale, was asked to present a plan he used in counciling with businesses.

The professor discussed a plan for determining long-range objectives, using the results of the retreat as input for the discussions. He suggested that the council determine six to eight broad objectives for Midvale. Each committee would then take these broad objectives and develop more specific objectives for its committee, using the broad objectives as a framework in which to operate.

After the committees defined their specific objectives, the council would review them and determine priorities of objectives for the coming year.

Next trained leaders from the congregation would meet with small groups of congregational members to discuss the objectives and priorities. Input from these meetings would then be fed back to the committees.

Finally the council would approve the objectives and priorities developed by the committees after considering the input from the small group meetings.

Three council members and the pastors developed the first set of broad objectives, which were then modified by the total council.

The objectives developed for Midvale Community Lutheran Church were as follows:

"To honor God by accepting the Gospel of Jesus Christ and sharing in word and action the love of God with each other, our community, and the world" by:

1. *Confronting* persons with God and what He has done for men through Jesus Christ, and to invite the response of faith, hope, and love *to God and all men.*

2. *Nurturing* all age groups in their continued Christian growth.

3. *Providing* opportunity for creation of Christian fellowship.

4. *Encouraging* participation in the community and the world as God's servants.

5. *Relating* Midvale's program to the events of the day in the light of God's revelation.

These were the objectives each church committee used as a framework for developing more specific objectives in their area of responsibility.

Adult Education Committee Determines Objectives. One of Midvale's committees is Adult Education. The following procedure[1] was used by the Adult Education Committee to develop its specific goals (other church committees used the same procedure).

1. *Identify the major work areas for the committee.* In a brain-storming session, three minutes was allowed for committee members to mention as many functions for the adult education committee as they could. They listed what they were now doing, and what they thought they should be doing. When the three minutes were up, committee members compared the list of work areas they noted with the printed list of functions for their committee.

2. *Set tentative priorities.* Committee members then discussed the work areas: (a) what they must do, (b) what they should do, and (c) what they could or could not do depending on resources, and whether or not (a) and (b) were accomplished.

3. *Discuss the priorities of work areas.* The committee members focused on what was to be accomplished by each work area. At this point, the Adult Education Committee looked at several sources of information to help decide what it should accomplish and the priorities it wished to determine.

The potential adult education participant himself was one source of information. Several techniques for determining participant interest were used. Informally, members of the adult education planning committee talked to church members to learn of their adult education interests. Various kinds of check lists and surveys were used.

The committee discussed what is known about the problems and needs adults have as they live through the stages in their lives. The developmental task framework explained in Chapter 3 offers some information about adult problems. For example, young adults have problems in rearing children, finding social groups, and so on. Middle-age adults often have problems relating to teenage children, accepting and adjusting to the physiological changes of middle age, etc. Other adults are adjusting to decreasing physical strength, adjusting to retirement, and maintaining relationships with others their own age.

The committee also used background information about the congregation, the number of people in different age groups, something about the occupations of members, the nature of the community surrounding the church, etc., as a basis for discussion.

4. *Write objectives.* The following guidelines were used in writing objectives:

   a. The objective is written starting with a "to" with an action verb. For example, an objective for the adult education committee might be: To increase the participation in the adult education program by 20 percent during the coming year.

   b. A single result is indicated in each objective.

   c. A target date for the accomplishment of the objective is indicated. Three levels of target dates may be considered: long-range objectives—two or more years to achieve; intermediate objectives—one to two years to achieve; and short-range objectives—one month, three months, nine months to achieve.

   d. Objectives should be short and simple.

   e. What and when are spelled out in the objective.

   f. The objectives are agreed on willingly by those who develop them.

   g. Some of the objectives should be new and innovative, something the committee hasn't done before.

   h. The number of objectives developed by each committee should be limited to four or five.

5. *Test objectives.* Test against the above criteria.

6. *Reach agreement.* Agree on the objectives and the priority given to them.

Following are the objectives determined by Midvale's Adult Education Committee after they worked through the above process.

Objectives for Midvale's Adult Education Program.
1. To increase awareness of how the Lutheran Church relates to basic issues of the day.
2. To increase understanding of biblical sources.
3. To increase knowledge of contemporary, historical, and theological concepts.

Sub-Objectives.
1. To provide Christian adult education opportunities on Sunday mornings.
2. To develop and provide learning opportunities for a minimum of five small study-discussion groups.
3. To coordinate and work with individual members or organizations of the church in education efforts.
4. To promote family-group education opportunities.

The above is one approach to determine objectives for an adult education program. It isn't an ideal plan and it won't fit every church's situation. There are other approaches that may be used, and this approach may be modified. I shared the approach with you to show how one church has done it. There may be elements in the plan that appeal to you and which fit your situation.

Of paramount importance in planning church adult education programs is having an idea of what you wish to accomplish. And for the adult education program to know what it wishes to accomplish the entire church must be aware of its goals.

Determining the goals of the adult education program is phase one. Next we will consider: selecting learning approaches, selecting learning experiences and teaching methods, and evaluating the adult education program.

6

Providing Learning Opportunities

There are many ways to organize adult education programs in the church. I'll talk about three broad approaches and then give specific examples of how each can be implemented.

APPROACHES TO LEARNING

The three approaches I'll discuss are: (1) learning as acquiring content, (2) learning as inquiry, and (3) learning as problem solving. For each approach, I'll try to relate the function of content, the function of the leader or instructor, and the function of learner. For all three, the primary focus is on the learner himself.

Learning As Acquiring Content

This is an approach that assumes there is an inherent value in the content for the learner. The learner wishes to do something that requires he know specific content, yet he doesn't know precisely what he needs to know and where he can get the information he needs. The content may be in a variety of forms—written materials, films, programmed learning kits, content the leader may have, content resource persons may have, mass-media content. In a general sense the learner has a particular need to acquire certain content and the instructor or leader helps the learner to acquire it.

Learning As Inquiry

Here the focus is on the relationship of the learner to a given content. The value of the content will vary from person to person based on the person's individual needs. The leader's function is to provide a setting where the learner can relate to the content in such a way that the content makes sense to the learner and has a unique value to him. The leader helps the learner identify component parts in the content, detect relationships among the parts, and determine the role played by each part of the content. Hopefully, the leader's function will decrease as the learner becomes more proficient in relating to the content.

The function of the learner in this approach is to relate to the content so the content has value to him personally. The aim of this approach isn't only clarification and accumulation of content, but encouragement and guidance of a process of discovery on the part of the learner. The leader and the textbook cease to be authoritative sources of content to be learned, but become, along with other sources of content, materials to be dissected and analyzed.

The emphasis isn't on the content for content's sake, but what the content is about, or, more specifically, how the content relates to the learner. This approach suggests a close relationship of the learner to the content, with the leader serving primarily as a guide in the process of inquiry.

Learning As Problem Solving

Here I'm talking about real-life problems people face, not a problem contrived by the leader who already knows the answer. I'm talking about problems that relate to the learner's family, his job, his relationships with his fellow man and the larger society, his concern for problems in the community.

In this approach, the function of the content is to help solve the problem the learner brings to the learning situation. The learner's function is to identify his problem, search for reasonable solutions, and finally settle on a solution to his problem.

The leader helps the learner define the problem, aids in the search for solutions, and, in many instances, is one source of content to the learner in his search for solutions.

There's considerable risk taking in this learning model—the problem may be difficult to isolate, and solution to the learner's problem is often not clearly apparent to either the leader or to the learner. Thus, there's a sharing in the learning transaction between the learner and the leader.

Occasionally, there may be no solution to the learner's problem—another risk the leader must be willing to assume.

SELECTING A LEARNING APPROACH

Obviously, the process of learning may be thought about in many ways—these are simply three ways that make sense to me. There is overlap among all three of the approaches—for a learner to participate in problem solving he has to acquire content. And for that content to be most useful in solving his problem, inquiry of that content is important.

Those responsible for planning contemporary church adult education programs have a problem in knowing which of these learning approaches is most applicable in a particular setting. It's not an easy question to answer. The planner of adult education programs must come back to the basic question: What is the purpose of this learning, with this adult, in this situation? Answering this question will help clarify which learning approach is most appropriate.

The following example, using the content area of sex education, explains the relationship of the three learning approaches and how the adult education planner decides which approach is most appropriate. Trained advisors for church youth groups often counsel with young people on sex education questions. An adult educator responsible for organizing learning experiences for these youth group advisors might decide, after talking with experienced pastors, consulting with experts in the field of sex education, and so on, that there are certain content areas these advisors should know before they'll be able to do even minimal counseling with young people. Here, I'd suggest the learning approach of acquiring content is appropriate.

A group of experienced youth advisors who regularly counsel on sex education questions would be treated differently. For this group, learning as problem solving is a more appropriate approach. The experienced advisors come to the learning situation with many unanswered questions that are real problems to them. They're searching for answers from many sources. The adult education leader helps the experienced advisors identify their problems in the area of sex education counseling and then helps them in their search for content to answer their questions. Outside resource persons, reading materials, and a sharing of answers by the participants themselves are all content sources.

We could also think about the same group of experienced youth advisors and the content area of sex education using the learning-as-inquiry approach. Using this approach, the adult education leader would help the advisors relate to the various kinds of sex education content available—analyzing it, learning something about the authors, the validity and reliability of the research that contributed to the content. Emphasis isn't on solving advisors' problems in relation to counseling about sex education, but helping them relate more personally to the content available.

Obviously overlap occurs among the three learning approaches.

When focusing on the problem-solving approach to counseling problems in sex education, the adult education leader helps the advisors in the process of inquiry as they look at various available content sources that may contribute to solving problems.

And using the example of the new advisors, they too could be directed in the process of inquiry as they deal with the content they must have to get started in counseling in the area of sex education.

As you think about the three learning approaches, you'll see other ways that they overlap and indeed become part of each other. The overlap really doesn't matter. What's important is knowing which learning model fits which learners and which content at a given time.

In the following chapters, I'll present case studies of adult education programs used by various churches throughout the country. I've tried to categorize the case studies according to the three learning approaches so you'll have a better understanding of the approaches and so you'll have some program ideas that you may wish to try.

LEARNING OPPORTUNITIES

So far I've discussed determining the purpose and direction of the adult education program and selecting learning approaches to meet the needs identified.

We're now ready to look at providing learning opportunities—the third phase in the programming process.

There are unlimited ways of providing opportunities for adults to learn. Here are several guideline questions to ask when selecting learning opportunities:

1. Will the participant know what he's trying to do? Will he understand the assignment?
2. Does the learning opportunity provide for involvement of the participant?
3. Will the participant be interested enough to try it?
4. Will he be able to do it?
5. Will he get feedback, some indication of how things are going, how well he's doing?
6. Will he get satisfaction? Doing something well will give more satisfaction than doing something poorly.
7. Are there enough learning opportunities available so the participant will have a chance to learn?

Following are several methods that can provide learning opportunities. At the end of the chapter I've listed several references that describe these methods in greater detail and also introduce additional methods.

Small Group Discussion

Four to six people meet at the same time to list questions or problems or suggest solutions to problems. They may meet as segments of a larger group or by themselves. The advantages of small group discussion are: (1) it's satisfying for group members, (2) it provides a situation where each feels free to take part, (3) members help each other increase flow of ideas, and (4) it develops teamwork.

Large Group Discussion

The entire group, no more than 25 or 30, discusses opinions, questions, or issues related to a particular topic.

The session may be structured with preplanned questions or it may be unstructured. Many of the same advantages for the small group discussion apply to the large group, although obviously there is less opportunity for involvement.

How the leader asks questions is the key to effective large group discussion. Some guidelines for asking questions are:

1. Avoid asking yes or no questions; use questions that begin with how, why, and which.

2. Ask the question before you call on someone to answer it. Not knowing who's expected to answer gets everyone thinking about the answer.

3. Avoid asking questions that suggest their own answers.

4. Questions that come from group members can often be turned back to the group. This often triggers additional discussion.

Panel Discussion

This is a group meeting where a moderator and a panel of two to eight expert members, representing different viewpoints, presents an impromptu discussion of a topic. Its primary advantages are to present many sides to a problem and bring out wide knowledge and experience.

A panel doesn't provide for a systematic presentation of a topic. Many questions are left only partially answered and usually panel members don't know in advance what questions will be raised. Therefore, the panel is better suited to presenting opinions than fact.

Role Playing

This method uses the members of the group as participants. They are asked to play act themselves, another designated person, or two persons may exchange roles and play each other. No preparation before the meeting of the group is allowed, thus the role playing is completely impromptu.

The primary purpose of role playing is help develop a better understanding of human behavior. The major advantages are: (1) developing understanding of the feelings of people, (2) developing understanding of the forces in a situation that block good human relations, and (3) getting the other fellow's point of view and situation.

Lecture

One qualified person presents a topic at a formal group meeting. This is an efficient way to present one side of a problem, bring new knowledge to a group, or provide background for group discussion. The major advantages are: (1) enables one person to present ideas to a large number of people, (2) makes a systematic presentation of ideas possible, (3) enables a person to get a great deal of information. The major disadvantages are: (1) members of the group retain only a small portion of the information presented, (2) group members usually don't become involved, and (3) few lecturers can hold the interest of a group for long.

Contract Group

This is a variation of small group discussion, where from 6 to 12 people come together and make a contract with each other that they'll attend "x" number of sessions, promise to read the agreed on assignments, commit themselves to attending all the meetings, and then agree to disband after a given time.

The major advantages of the contract group are: (1) the group members have a mutual commitment to each other for learning, (2) close human relationships develop that carry beyond the contract group meetings, (3) group members feel a responsibility toward helping fellow members if they have problems, supporting each other in time of need, etc.

Reading Assignments

This method is often overlooked with adult groups because assigned readings may remind some participants of their formal school years. But acquiring information by reading remains one of the best and most efficient learning methods. The learner can progress at his own speed, he can read when he has time, and he has the written word to refer back to if he has questions. The major disadvantage is the problem of motivation. Some persons aren't motivated to learn by themselves; they need the support and encouragement of the group. But for many people reading is an important learning method.

These are but seven kinds of teaching methods; there are many more: field trips, dialogue, symposium, interviews, illustrated talks, method demonstration, exhibits.

BEHAVIORAL OBJECTIVES

When preparing to use a particular method or methods, the adult education planner often asks: "Do I need to write behavioral objectives?" The need for predetermined behavioral objectives has become an issue among adult educators in recent years.

Can adult education programs in the church be run without behavioral objectives? Earlier I discussed objectives for the church and objectives for a church's adult education program. There is no question that these kinds of objectives must be determined and made known. But behavioral objectives are different.

Behavioral objectives are commonly thought of as

statements that indicate what behavioral change is expected in the learner as a result of participating in an adult education activity. They're usually written to indicate: (1) who is the learner, (2) what is the subject matter, and (3) what behavioral change is expected. The expected behavioral change refers to change in knowledge or what the person knows, a change in attitude or what the person feels or believes, or a change in skills or what the person is able to do.

Many educators suggest that before any instructional program commences, the behavioral objectives must be written. The reasoning is that the behavioral objectives will serve as guidelines for the leader as he plans his instructional program. The leader can make decisions about what learning opportunities can best accomplish which objectives, what instructional aids are necessary such as audio-visual materials or written materials, and of course what subject-matter content will best contribute to achieve the objectives.

It is also argued that the behavioral objectives can serve as a bench mark against which the leader can measure whether or not learning has taken place. The rationale is: the leader knows what behavioral change is expected, evaluation is thus only a matter of devising a measuring tool to determine the extent to which the behavioral objective was reached.

There's a major problem with dependence on behavioral objectives as a requisite to learner involvement. In my opinion, it's an error to believe that before every adult education program, there needs to be a long list of behavioral objectives. I believe this for several reasons.

1. Learning approaches are not all the same. I've described three learning approaches—learning as problem solving, learning as inquiry, and learning as acquiring content. Predetermination of behavioral objectives fits but one approach . . . learning as acquiring content.

The behavioral objective route to learning makes the process of learning seem very simple, simple to the point that all learning situations can be structured in the same way. The process of predetermining behavioral objectives suggests that first you discover the need. Then you write behavioral objectives to meet that need, you search for content and learning experiences to meet the objectives, subject the intended learner to the planned learning opportunities, and finally decide whether the behavioral objectives you wrote earlier were met. It's a neat, step-by-step, well-organized package. But I would argue that learning isn't that simple. You can't look at every person, or group of persons, and use the same structured approach to meet their needs and solve their problems.

2. Predetermining behavioral objectives violates several learning guidelines I mentioned in Chapter 3. Behavioral objectives can't be written, in the majority of instances, for a group of people. It's extremely unlikely that each behavioral objective will fit every member of that group. As I said in Chapter 3, learning must focus on the needs and problems of the individual to be effective. When behavioral objectives are written for each individual, with that person involved in developing the objectives, the focus on the individual learner is preserved. Behavioral objectives written for groups of people violate the "individual-focus" emphasis.

Predetermined behavioral objectives also violate the learning guideline of actively involving the learner in making decisions about what is to be learned, how it is to be learned, and whether learning has occurred.

And finally, predetermined behavioral objectives violate the guideline that the learner is a source of ideas. When behavioral objectives are predetermined, the learner is overlooked as a rich source of content that can contribute to the learning situation.

There are times when behavioral objectives are important and should be used, but there are also times when they're not appropriate. When there's content that a learner needs to know to do something, then behavioral objectives can be important tools. But for other approaches to learning, when acquisition of subject matter or content isn't the focus, predetermined behavioral objectives may hinder the process of learning.

In the next two chapters we shall look at three approaches to learning in greater detail: learning as inquiry, as problem solving, and as acquiring content.

7

Learning as Inquiry

Learning as inquiry is probably the most popular approach to learning churches use. You'll recall that this is the approach where the learner comes in contact with a particular subject matter or content. Each person gets something different from the experience based on his background of experience and his needs and interests.

The leader's role is helping the learner better understand the content, helping him with a procedure for studying the content, and helping him select various types of content

Following are several content sources and how they can be used in an adult education program. In many instances, I've used actual case studies of programs local churches have conducted using a particular content source.

Films and Filmstrips

The Parish of the Immaculate Conception Catholic Church in New Richmond, Wisconsin, conducted an adult education series on world problems. They borrowed several filmstrips from the Christian Renewal Center (Rice Lake, Wisconsin) on such topics as poverty, social injustice, and war. After the presentation of these filmstrips, the group of about 50 was divided into groups of 10 to discuss the church's role in these world problems.

The University Baptist Church, State College, Pennsylvania, conducted a 10-week film series, films of about 10 to 30 minutes, on such topics as the nature of man, the present religious search, and forms of mission. Following the film, people met in small groups, and with a leader and study guide explored the meaning of the film.

Midvale Lutheran Church in Madison, Wisconsin, organized a group of people to attend the film "Guess Who's Coming to Dinner". Following the film, the group met at the church, and using a study guide discussed the film.

Films and filmstrips are thus one excellent source of content that may be used by church adult education groups. For films to be of greatest value, the discussion leader should have a series of questions in mind that will help the participants remember and understand the film.

Some questions that may be asked are:

1. What was the theme of the film?
2. What was the film trying to say?
3. Were there parts of the film that shocked you?
4. Who were the major characters and how did they contribute to the story?
5. Who were the minor characters and what was their contribution?
6. What disappointed you about the film?
7. What one or two things did you learn from the film?
8. How did you feel while you watched the film?

9. Did you have feelings before the film that changed after watching it?

10. How does what you saw in the film relate to any real-life experiences you've had?

If the group leader has an opportunity to preview the film, he can develop additional, specific questions about the film.

In any discussion of a film, the questions should be used as discussion starters, not as a structure that must be adhered to—first we answer question 1 and then we go on to 2. There must be a balance from no organization or direction in the discussion, where people may get off on a topic quite unrelated to the film, to the overstructed discussion where there's only recitation of answers.

Another approach to film viewing may be for small listening groups to organize before the film is viewed. One or two questions are assigned to each group and then following the viewing each listening group reports on its answers to the total group.

A possible danger with this approach is that people watching for specifics may not see the more subtle, broader kinds of messages certain films may have.

Folk Music as Content

Folk music may be overlooked as content for religious adult education groups . . . yet it's a rich source.

The First Baptist Church of Newton, Massachusetts, used folk music in an interesting way as a part of an adult education series conducted on communications. Each person in the group was given a mimeographed copy of the words for "Who Will Answer?" by Ed Ames. The recording was played as the group members silently followed the words. Group members were then asked to reflect, to themselves, the answer to the question: What does this song say to us? What does it say about our belief in the "living God?" What can you say to the questioner?

Members of the group were asked to read from Philippians 2: 12b, 13. To keep the verse in context, they were encouraged to read several passages that come before and after the one assigned. For about 15 minutes, group members were asked to study the Bible passage and meditate on it. They were then asked to write what they heard God saying through the passage to them about the here and now. More specifically, they were asked to write answers to the question: What truth is this passage bringing to you? Where is this truth working in my life? What new possibilities does it suggest to me? What person or situation does this passage help me to see differently? What are some possibilities for my own growth?

Each member of the group then read aloud his "truth" and the other group members told him what they found interesting and important. Group members were encouraged to ask questions to help the individual clarify or develop his ideas, or what he was thinking of when he wrote them. Judgments about what a person was saying were ruled out. Following this, the entire group listened again to the recording "Who Will Answer?"

In this case, folk music and Bible study were combined. Folk music may be used alone as content for discussion by a group, and questions discussed like: What is the folk singer saying? What are the basic ideas he is trying to express? What is the relationship of his ideas to the church?

Often folk singers raise basic questions: Who an I? What should I become? What is my relationship to the world? To other people? Rather than supplying religious answers, folk music may often be a source of questions for further discussion. In this way, it can be a stimulus.

The Resource Person as Content

Many churches use outside resource people as contributions to adult education programs. Used properly, the input can be useful and exciting. Used improperly, the resource person may only be entertainment under the guise of religious adult education.

Before you can decide for or against asking resource persons you must ask: What am I trying to accomplish with this adult education program? Can a resource person help accomplish my purpose? What can a resource person do that couldn't be accomplished another way? Careful thought about these questions will help solve the problem of yes or no a resource person.

There are many instances in your religious adult education programming when a resource person may be the most appropriate means to accomplish what you and your group want to accomplish. A resource person may be the answer if you:

1. Need factual information that isn't readily available, or factual material that must be interpreted before it is useful.

2. Need someone to share personal experiences that can't effectively be presented in another way.

Asking the Resource Person

Plan ample lead time when inviting a resource person—six weeks to two months or longer, if possible. This will give him adequate time to prepare for the assignment. Also, if the first person you select can't participate, there'll be time to invite an alternative.

Make certain you indicate to the resource person exactly what contribution you want him to make. He should know the purpose of your program. Before contacting the person have clearly in mind how you are structuring the program to gain most from his participation.

69

A resource person doesn't always give a speech. He may answer questions that a panel or group of members pose to him. Or he may give a short talk and then respond to questions from the group. If the latter format is followed, it's important that group members be prepared to raise pertinent questions so the resource person can be used effectively. If you expect the resource person to deliver a prepared speech, indicate it to him and the length of speech expected.

Provide the resource person with some background information about the group—how large it is, the kinds of experiences the group has had in the area you are asking him to make a contribution, the age range of the group, and who he should contact when he arrives.

Determine if the speaker expects payment for his presentation and expense money for travel.

The Resource Person with Your Group

When he arrives, introduce the resource person individually to the early arrivers so he can get some feel for the group.

And when you introduce him formally to the group indicate something about his qualifications relative to the topic and the contribution you expect him to make to the class. This will help the group focus on what they are to accomplish at this session. Also indicate to the group the plan you have for using the resource person as a reminder to the group of what you planned earlier.

Printed Material as Content

Books and other printed material are popular inputs for adult discussion groups, and if properly used can trigger useful learning. To be most useful, there must be planning of how the materials will be used with the group. Lon Speer in *Creative Procedures for Adult*

Groups, Harold D. Minor, ed., suggests a procedure to use where the reading is done as part of the group activity. His procedure involves five steps.

Step 1: Read and Outline. Students are asked to number all the paragraphs in the chapter, bulletin, or whatever they're to read. They're asked to read the entire chapter for overall meaning, then to read it paragraph by paragraph to capture the main point in each paragraph. Each participant should have a sheet of paper numbered to correspond with the number of paragraphs. For each paragraph, the main idea is written in one sentence.

The participants are asked to read their summary sentences and group them into blocks of thought or major ideas. A chapter with 50 paragraphs may have 5 to 10 major ideas.

Step 2: Recall. Using their outlines, the participants indicate to each other what they've read. One or two people may share their group's major thought with other participants. No attempts to evaluate or judge what has been read should be made at this point.

Step 3: Interpret. In their own words, the participants try to say what the writer is saying. But again there should be no attempt at evaluation.

Step 4: Evaluate. Now personal reactions to the material are invited. There's discussion about whether the writer is thought right or wrong, who agrees with him and who doesn't.

Step 5: Application. At this point in the discussion the words of the writer and the experiences of the participants should be coming together. If the experience has been successful what has been discussed is being internalized by the participants. The amount and the kind of internalization will of course vary from one participant to another.

To some persons this procedure will seem mechanical and boring. Others may not be able to hold off evaluating the material as they proceed through steps 1, 2, and 3. Yet the basis for this approach is an understanding of what is written before it's evaluated.

Inadequate understanding of what is written often leads to difficulty when groups discuss written material. Worse yet, the discussion is valueless if a large proportion of the group members haven't read the material at all. You may not want to use the approach outlined above with all groups and with all written material. But for a group that hasn't had experience discussing written material, it may be a useful procedure to try.

Perhaps we need to provide reading time as a part of our discussion of written materials. Some groups may welcome this opportunity and thus be more profitable as learning groups. Other groups may wish to do their reading at home and would see this as a needless exercise taking away from more profitable interaction.

Content from a Combination of Sources

So far, I've talked about content from specific sources to be used by learning groups in the church. But often courses are organized that combine several of the content sources, films with books plus resource people, for example.

St. John's Lutheran Church, Summit, New Jersey, conducted a program which combined books and films. Specific members of the parish were selected by the staff to be discussion leaders for the specific topics. Participants were urged to read the books and view the films before the discussion. The methods used in teaching were dialogue (between adults and youth), questions and answers, and sharing of specific feelings.

Another adult education program conducted at St. Johns included about 15 persons from the parish involved in a Christian art group. They made banners, title mosaics, processional crosses, and various items of interpretation, using copper, stained glass, and casting plaster. The core of this program was a study of various signs and symbols of the church before using these items in the area of interpretation. The group included adults and youth.

The First United Methodist Church of Glendale, California, also used a combination of content sources in its adult education program "Project Understanding." A five-Sunday program was planned with the following objectives:

1. To bring blacks and whites into actual physical contact in an acceptable setting.

2. Help them see one another as persons.

3. Experience the scope of redemption rather than just talk about it.

The sources of content for contemporary church adult education programs are limitless. I've tried in this chapter to give a number of examples of how various sources of content may be used, hoping that the suggestions will trigger many more ideas.

With limitless sources of content, the challenge is to organize the learning activities so the participants can react to and interact with the materials. Just exposure to new ideas isn't enough . . . the participants must have the opportunity to internalize the ideas in such a way that it becomes a part of the participants. It's only when this occurs that learning takes place.

8

Solving Problems and Acquiring Content

LEARNING AS PROBLEM SOLVING

Every person has problems . . . in his work, with his spouse, understanding his children. Problem-solving learning focuses on helping the learner solve his problems. The learner doesn't come to an adult education session simply because he wants to become more familiar with a particular subject—he comes because he has a problem and he believes the session may help.

The focus of learning as inquiry (Chapter 7) is on the subject matter and the relationship of the person to that subject matter. But the focus for learning as problem solving is on the problems that people have.

Thus, learning as problem solving must be organized differently and conducted differently than learning as inquiry. In the initial planning stages, an attempt must be made to determine what problems people have.

Let's look at an example. Several people mentioned understanding their teenage sons and daughters was a problem for them, and they agreed to attend a series of sessions to deal with this problem. Let's assume that you're responsible for organizing the sessions.

Rather than plan in detail each of the sessions, the first meeting of the group can be a planning meeting. Involving the group members in making decisions about future direction will help ensure that the problems people have are being discussed.

Involving Members in Planning

Here some techniques you can use to involve the group in planning succeeding sessions. Before the group meets for the first time, contact the people who have signed up. Ask them to bring with them to the first meeting a list of questions they have about understanding their teenagers. Some won't take time to write a list of questions before coming to the first meeting, but the contact will start them thinking about the topic.

At the first meeting, after everyone has been introduced, you're ready to explore with them the specifics of what they want to discuss in the following sessions. You can indicate that the sessions will be built around what they've identified as problem areas and questions. Make certain the group understands that the remaining sessions haven't all been planned and that what you're asking isn't simply an exercise.

Following the introductory remarks, break the larger group into smaller groups of five or six each. Ask each group to discuss and be prepared to report on at least three problem areas or questions they would like to have answered in coming meetings. Give them a specific time limit to do this, perhaps ten minutes. When using this technique it's essential for each small group to know its assignment exactly and how much time it has to accom plish its task.

Following the 10 minutes of small group discussion

ask each group to report the problems and questions they've identified. The first group might report.

1. How can we keep our teenagers interested in attending church?
2. How are mass media affecting our youth?
3. What are the effects of drinking and drugs on teenagers today?-

As the groups report, write the questions on the board or a flip chart. Get similar reports from the other groups and write these questions on the board. Your role as group leader then becomes one of refining and sharpening the questions that are written on the board. You do this by asking questions of the groups, summarizing responses to these questions, and relating questions raised from various groups.

You may ask, "What do you want to know about mass media affecting our youth? Which mass media? Affecting them in what way? How does it affect them? When does it affect them?" The group that raised this problem area is forced to think more deeply about the question. Someone from that group may respond, "Well, I guess we were most concerned about the suggestive magazines and books we find on the newsstand. It's our feeling that this sort of trash can't help but affect our kids in an adverse way. But we'd like to know more about it. We'd like to know just how serious the problem is."

You, as group leader, can probe and relate until you have a list of specific questions that might be considered as topics for the coming meetings. You'll probably have listed many more questions than could possibly be considered in the number of sessions the group has agreed on. If this is so, then you need to develop a priority with the group about which questions they feel are most important for discussion at this time.

Avoid trying to include something in the coming sessions that relates to each question; rather, help the group develop a list of the most pressing concerns. You may decide to consider one question at each session, or one question may be the concern of several sessions.

Through this process, you've helped the group identify the areas within the broad topic of "Understanding Your Teenager" that are the most relevant to the concerns of the class members. The group members have been involved in the process, so motivation should be high and will remain high as the group considers questions they want answered.

Group Leader as Guide

Your role as group leader is one of guide. You guide the members into defining the problems to be considered. Your next task is to help find appropriate materials and resources that will help answer the questions that have been identified. The resources may be written materials, films, outside resource people, and of course you can't overlook that participants in the group may have answers to some of the questions.

Your task is to organize the sessions so that the participants can interact with the resources and with each other so they're able to find solutions to their problems. Here too, you continue to serve as a guide, raising questions, offering suggestions, but not serving as an authoritarian source of answers.

The focus of this learning approach is on the individual learner and his problems, not on the content to be presented. By using this approach, you'll be dealing with the real problems of the participants, not with problems someone else thinks are problems.

Here's an example of a problem-solving situation reported by Joseph E. Taylor, Minister, Trinity United Methodist Church, Little Rock, Arkansas.

> In a small city in the deepest part of the Mississippi Delta, where problems are plenteous and solu-

tions scarce (and generally unpopular), a group of young adults decided what they were studying was irrelevant. Their curricular material often touched on the problems associated with race, but usually in an oblique manner. They were living in an area where every vestige of culture and "order" as they had known it was in constant peril of being shattered. They knew some solutions to the tensions in which they were living had to be found, and soon, or explosion was inevitable.

They were aware, as are most young adults today, that there are other problems too. They were concerned about Viet Nam in particular and war in general.

A small group of them got together with the minister and talked—and talked. Finally some decisions were reached. Among these were:

1. We need to meet together some time other than Sunday morning.

2. We need at least a couple of hours per session.

3. We need to invite a larger number of young adults not presently active in Church School.

4. We need an issue-oriented study.

5. We need to develop an atmosphere where we can really take off our gloves and remove our masks, and talk straight.

6. We need some biblical background if we are going to have a perspective from which to tackle these problems.

The group made some tentative decisions:

1. We would meet on Saturday evenings in the homes of members of the group.

2. We would invite others on a personal, almost social basis, to our homes.

3. The atmosphere was to be as open and free as we could make it.

4. We would begin studying a book in the Bible which seemed to come to grips with problems in

the day it was written. We choose the Corinthian correspondence.

5. We would keep the focus on today and our problems, using the Scripture as resource material.

6. We would not prepare any roll and wouldn't plan on continuing for any set time.

The first few sessions were pretty much social. We later decided that this was probably inevitable. We were getting used to each other and to a new setting.

As weeks passed, the reserve and pretense of participants went down sharply. We began to wrestle with feelings and prejudices, and resentments. We got so we could talk about virtually anything and hear each other.

The results, aside from statistical growth, phenomenal regularity of attendance, etc., were not easy to assess. Where we began to see progress, though, was quite outside the church itself. These young men and women were leaders in many community and civic groups. They found themselves starting discussions and making comments which actually startled them. They found that their willingness to talk about the problems we are living in, made it easier for others to do the same.

In official meetings in the church new voices began to be heard. Old policies were brought into question, many for the first time. Some were changed.

This group lasted about 18 months. Transfers, moves, etc., took their toll and before it had lost its identity, the group agreed to disband and look for another setting.

Conditions for Problem Solving

This example points out several crucial conditions for effective problem-solving:

1. The problems discussed must be the problems of the participants, not someone else's problems.

2. There must be heavy involvement of the participants in making decisions about problems to be

discussed, and also the way the group will organize and function.

3. There is a certain element of risk for the group leader. In this example the group leader was concerned about the early meetings being primarily social. A less secure person might have been concerned enough to not allow the group to proceed as it was and destroy the atmosphere that was developing. In a problem-solving, learning situation there must be flexibility and freedom, and the outcomes aren't always those the group leader feels should occur.

4. There is little structure and organization. The group is organized enough so they know when they will meet and what they will be discussing. How they will participate is left to the group members.

5. There is no sense of failure when a group disbands. If a group is truly problem solving, it should be expected that when the problems identified are solved as best they can be, the group feels a sense of accomplishment and quits. Later members of the group may organize again, with others, to work on problems not yet identified. Meeting for the sake of meeting is avoided in the problem-solving group.

LEARNING AS ACQUIRING CONTENT

There are times in programming for religious adult education when the focus must be on the content and specific learning to be accomplished by participants.

Let me share a rather obvious example. As a part of their social action programs, many churches encourage members to volunteer services in hospitals, children's homes, and so on. Obviously, before these people can be effective they must know something about the duties of their volunteer positions. Often the institutions where they'll work will provide much of this orientation assistance, but the church has a role too. What is a Christian's role in assisting an institution such as a children's home? What action should a church take to support such institutions in a community? These are questions for a church adult education group. And obviously the people who are most interested are those who serve as volunteers in various institutions.

Now let's look at planning adult education where the focus is on acquiring some specific content. The major difference between this approach to learning, and learning as problem solving, or learning as inquiry is the lesser amount of input the learner makes toward what is to be learned.

This is understandable. If someone has never worked in a children's home before, he has little basis for knowing what he should learn about children's homes. He relies on others who are more experienced with the content to organize and plan the learning activities. Someone from the home may meet with those who know little about the organization and its operation. They may visit the home to see the program in action. Those who lack understanding of little children may be given a variety of reading materials, they may be shown films, they may have a chance to interact with someone who knows little children well.

The focus of this learning approach isn't on the problems of the participant, but on what the learner needs to know to do something. As the organizer of this approach to learning, you must first be concerned with what specifically needs to be learned, then assist the learner in determining the extent to which he already knows and can do what is required. Finally you must make a variety of learning experiences available to the learner.

A mistake that's often made when this approach to learning is considered is assuming that all the participants are at the same level of understanding. When this assumption is made, the adult education programmer often includes all of the participants in all of the learning experiences. This of course violates the idea of individualizing instruction to account for individual participant difference and need.

9

Evaluating Adult Education Programs

The last stage in the program development process is evaluation. Indeed it's an error to refer to evalution as the "last stage." It's a part of the program development process that should be going on all the time, before the program commences, during the operation of the program, and at the end of the program.

Evaluation is variously defined as determining what you have accomplished, measuring whether your objectives have been met, and determining where you are compared with where you said you were going. A more refined definition of evaluation is judging the worth or value of an educational program according to some definite criteria and purposes.

According to Steele,[1] evaluation is never done just for its own sake but should contribute to the refinement of the present program or to the betterment of future programs.

"Evaluation should be a part of answering questions about the appropriateness of methods, content, and program approach . . . " [2] so educational programs can be continually improved.

Thus, evaluation is more than determining the value of the end product of your educational program. It's a means of learning something about current programs so changes can be made along the way.

Steele says three elements are necessary in educational program evaluation: (1) criteria, (2) evidence, and (3) judgment. The three elements are closely related to each other. An educational program is judged against criteria. The judgment is based on evidence collected about the extent to which the program met the criteria.

A number of check sheets can be used to get evidence from groups about educational programs. Some of the check sheets are useful in determining how the present program is going, some can help you get information about what the participants are learning, and some are most useful in providing clues for future programs.

SUNDAY MORNING ADULT EDUCATION EVALUATION
(Distributed at last session)

1. This past year I attended about the following number of Sunday morning adult education sessions. (Please check.)

    ——————— ¼
    ——————— ½
    ——————— ¾
    ——————— nearly all

2. Which Sunday morning adult education programs were *most* meaningful to you?

3. Which Sunday morning adult education programs were *least* meaningful to you?

4. What did you like *best* about the Sunday morning adult education series?

5. What did you like *least?*

6. What are your suggestions for improving the Sunday morning adult education series?

7. What suggestions do you have for future adult education programs?

A variety of useful evidence comes from an evaluation instrument like this. You can determine something about how the content was received, which approaches were most acceptable, and suggestions for improving both the approaches used and ideas for future programs.

But this type of check sheet provides little information about what was actually learned. The following evaluation form helps the program evaluator learn something about the learning that took place.

EVALUATION FORM

(Adult Education, Understanding My Teenager Series)

1. When I came to this course, I had hoped . . .

2. Now that I have taken the course, I feel . . .

3. A practical thing from the course which I plan to use is . . .

4. A suggestion I would like to make . . .

This form focuses on the participant's expectations and the extent to which his expectations were met with an adult education series. The form is concerned with the individual learner and his needs, and the extent to which those needs were met as seen by the participant himself.

The end of the meeting form can be used to measure participant reaction at the end of any given group session. It gives some indication of participant feelings about the meeting, what he felt was accomplished, the format used, and reaction to the group leader. Here is an example of one type of form that may be used.

END OF MEETING EVALUATION
(SMALL GROUP DISCUSSION)

(Please circle your rating)

	Rating				
	Low				High
1. How satisfied were you with this session?	1	2	3	4	5
2. To what extent did you feel comfortable in the group?	1	2	3	4	5
3. To what extent do you know the group members?	1	2	3	4	5
4. To what extent were your personal objectives met?	1	2	3	4	5
5. To what extent did you contribute to the discussion?	1	2	3	4	5
6. To what extent did the group stay on the announced topic?	1	2	3	4	5
7. I would rate the group leader	1	2	3	4	5

Suggestions:

Too often evaluation is overlooked or forgotten when adult education programs are planned and conducted. Or at best, someone voices his impressions of a particular adult education program and that serves as the evaluation.

Evaluation can be a useful tool to make changes in existing programs, to know if people are learning as a result of participating, and as a guide for the development of future programs.

10

Discussing Controversial Issues

There was a time when church-sponsored adult education avoided controversial subjects and all topics for discussion by adult groups were filtered through a "sweetness-and-light" screen.

Not so today. Many churches throughout the United States and Canada are taking a renewed interest in the community and social action. As a result they find themselves in the middle of one controversial issue after another, often with parishioners taking two or more sides.

When an adult group in a church wants to get involved, there's an excellent learning opportunity. As a springboard for discussion, controversial issues can serve as an impetus for education if the leader of the group is able to capitalize on the situation and its positive aspects.

POSITIVE OUTCOMES

Here are some of the positive things that can come out of discussions of controversial issues.

1. Often the issues most important to a community are controversial—open housing, student riots, hippies, police brutality, population control, interracial marriage. By taking one or more of these issues for discussion in its adult groups, the church underlines that it's a part of the community and that the community is a part of the church's concern. Moreover, when it refuses to stand aside while the issues of the day are being debated, the church also reaffirms that religion has something distinctive to contribute to the whole discussion.

2. Many men and women still don't believe adult education has anything to offer them, no matter who sponsors the program. However, when a discussion dealing with a controversial issue is presented, those who haven't previously attended adult education courses may turn out. "That's something we're interested in," they'll tell you. And once you get them coming, they are more apt to attend other kinds of adult education programs.

3. Because motivation is often high when adults attend sessions devoted to controversial issues, substantial learning often takes place. That high motivation prompts greater learning is a basic educational principle.

4. Within a congregation, often a few people will favor one side of a particular issue and an equally small number will favor the opposite side. The majority of the people have no feeling either way. Through an educational exposure to a particular issue, more adults will be in a position to decide where they stand. Thus through its educational program the church can help to develop a committed group of adults, even though on many issues more than one point of view will continue to be expressed. It's less disturbing when more than one opinion is held by members of a congregation than when many members simply hold no position at all on a particular issue.

5. The individual who thinks he understands an issue and knows his position on it also can benefit. Defending a position is one of the best ways to verify if you truly understand it. In fact, debate often generates new information for those involved. Thus, learning can occur for all parties, including those who listen to the debate.

These are only a few of the positive outcomes that can result from a discussion of controversial issues. But such outcomes don't occur automatically.

An educational leader should understand a number of things when working with an adult group in the discussion of controversial issues. No measured recipes exist, no step-by-step procedures can be prescribed—but there are some guidelines. If these are followed, it's more likely that you'll get positive outcomes when your group discusses issues having several points of view.

Guidelines for Controversial Discussions

As with any other learning experience in adult education, there must be planning for the experience to be effective.

Planning is especially important when dealing with controversial issues. You need to ask: What is to be accomplished as a result of the group's discussing this particular issue? Are we trying only to create an awareness of the issue? Or are we trying to get some resulting action on the part of the church members who participate?

Most effective planning is done when a small group of parishioners who are interested in a controversial issue sit down and talk about how a larger number can be involved. This group also tries to determine what outcomes should result from the experience, how many sessions should be held, whether resource people should be used at the sessions, when the sessions should be held, how the meetings will be publicized, what reading resources might be available. The group can then give its individual members specific assignments to get these jobs done.

When controversial issues are discussed, the disagreement must focus on the ideas involved and not on feelings toward the individuals putting forth these ideas.

No leader wants a discussion to end with a name-calling duel in which two or more participants become so emotionally involved that they can no longer talk objectively about the issues.

Here's an example. A black pastor from a Chicago church, along with four young parishioners, were invited to talk to a nearly all-white church in Madison, Wisconsin. The purpose of the session was to acquaint the white congregation with problems experienced by black youngsters as they grow up in a federal housing development. The pastor and his panel spent nearly an hour describing the situation, indicating some of their difficulties and the reasons why a federal housing unit wasn't the answer to all their problems. When they had finished, the meeting was opened to questions. The first questions were: How tall are these buildings you live in? Do you have to pay rent? How do you get to live in one of these units?

But then the questioning changed. Someone in the back of the room asked: "How come those housing units are always dirty? Why don't you people learn how to clean your homes? Then you wouldn't have so many problems."

Another listener jumped up and challenged the questioner. "You're just like all the rest of the people around here. Those people in Chicago don't have a chance to keep their places clean."

"What business is it of yours?" the first person retorted. "Why stick your nose into my question? Let the panelists try to answer for themselves."

"I stuck my nose in because your question is unfair, and I didn't want to embarrass our panel guests."

During this exchange, the two participants grew more and more angry, less and less able to face the issue.

Another example: A church group wanted to discuss the question of interracial marriage. When the film *Guess Who's Coming to Dinner* came to town, the group agreed to attend the screening and meet afterwards at the church to discuss it. The leader prepared some discussion questions on what the group had seen and what the film had meant to them. One of the questions was: What would you say to your son or daughter if he or she wanted to date someone from another race? After discussing some specifics of the film, the group got to the problem of how to deal with questions raised by their children. About half of the participants had teen-age children.

One woman started with: "Well, last night my daughter went to a dance with a Negro boy from her school. I think he's a fine young man. I didn't discourage her one bit."

"I could never allow that," someone else said. "I don't believe it's right for boys and girls of different races to date."

"Why don't you believe it's right?" another person asked.

"Well, I would be concerned that the person from another race couldn't support my daughter if they were to get married."

"Let's say he could support your daughter. Let's assume he came from a family that earned about the same income you do. What would you say then?"

"I don't know. I really hadn't thought about it quite that way before. I just assumed he wouldn't be able to make much money."

This was discussion of issues, not personalities, with people freely offering their opinions about various facets of the issue. There was obvious disagreement in the group. Some of the participants could see few problems with interracial dating, others thought it absolutely shouldn't be allowed, and still others didn't really know where they stood. But the group continued to keep the discussion focused on the issue.

You can avoid this problem altogether, of course, if the purpose of your session is for the group to have merely a passing awareness of an issue. For this, all you need is a guest speaker or a film. But assuming that you're trying to accomplish something more than this, how can you insure that your discussion will deal only with issues and not personalities?

One of the first things you can do is help group members get to know each other as people.

If you are striving for a discussion of problems that really concerns people, they have to become involved. The small-group type of discussion is one of the best ways to accomplish this.

The first time the group meets, they may spend time simply getting acquainted with each other and with the issue. This is a particularly good approach if they've agreed to spend several sessions discussing the subject. The best results will be obtained by dividing the group into small subgroups of six to eight people.

Have name tags for the participants and seat them in a circle so they can easily see each other. Foster informality; discourage people from standing or raising their hand when they speak. Begin by having each person give his name, something about his family, where he works, his church activities. Besides helping everyone get better acquainted, this self-introduction gets each person used to speaking to the group rather than to individual participants.

Many other techniques may be used in addition to the introductions which will help group members develop a comfortable, informal relationship with each other.

Lovers Lane United Methodist Church, Dallas, Texas, established a three-session series for Sunday mornings focusing on developing good group relationships. They chose to establish the series in preparation for participation in an interracial, youth day.

The first session focused on that which aided or hindered trust between persons. The group verbally dealt with the question and was at a standstill. Then group members participated in a trust-mistrust exercise in which one partner led his blindfolded partner and attempted to communicate through touch and feel. The exercise let the participants experience trust and mistrust, and sparked much discussion about the problem.

In the second session, the group used what they called "the-12-card-dialogue" method. The larger group was divided into smaller groups. Each smaller group was given a set of 12 cards, each having a related term printed on it. One card was left blank for the group to label as it saw fit. The groups were asked to arrange the cards according to the way they saw the terms related to one another. There was no "proper" arrangement. The value of the assignment was that as the group struggled for their card arrangement, they entered into significant dialogue. The group members found this technique exciting. They were amazed at the ideas that came from the group members themselves. They also saw how prone they were to search for the "right order." The exercise helped the group focus on the problem of people wanting "to be right," to conform, to be like others.

In the third week, each participant identified a concern or problem. Then he was asked to illustrate this concern or problem with a 12-inch piece of wire. This allowed group members to express themselves, to be creative, and to exchange interpretations of the created "wire symbols." This experience also helped the group see the tremendous ideas, creativity, and insight that was available to the group—if persons could give and take and be free and open.

Poor communications in discussion groups is often a problem when persons are discussing controversial issues. A person is so intent on thinking about an answer or a response to an argument another person has that he fails to hear what the other person is saying. Thus, the two people are talking past each other and the real issue of the discussion is often missed.

"Listening Triads" is an exercise a group may use to help individuals become more aware of and sharpen their listening skills. It works like this:

The larger group is broken into groups of three. In each small group (triad), one person is designated speaker, one listener, and one referee.

The discussion in the triad is unstructured except that the listener may not respond to the speaker until he first summarizes, in his own words and without notes, what the speaker has said.

The referee listens and interrupts if he feels the listener has incorrectly summarized what the speaker has said.

The speaker may choose one of several topics on which to speak, he may choose one of his own or he may choose from such topics as:

Is interracial and interfaith marriage good or bad? Why?

Is premarital sex relations acceptable or not? Why?

Is the Church as an institution dying? Why?

Why do so many people criticize the church?

After seven minutes of discussion by the speaker and the listener, the listener becomes the speaker, the speaker becomes referee, and the referee the listener. The new speaker is again allowed to choose a topic he wishes to discuss. The discussion continues again for seven minutes and another switch is made. All three members of the triad should have an opportunity to be speaker, listener, and referee.

When each has had an opportunity, the total group could discuss questions like:[1]

1. Did you find that you had difficulty in listening to others during the exercise? Why?

2. Did you find that you had difficulty formulating your thoughts and listening at the same time?
   a. Forgetting what you were going to say?
   b. Not listening to others?
   c. Rehearsing your response?

3. When others paraphrased your remarks, did they do it in a shorter, more concise way?

4. Did you find that you weren't getting across what you wanted to say?

5. Was the manner of presentation by others affecting your listening ability?

I have used this listening exercise with many groups and have had excellent results. Most people are surprised that they listen so poorly. And obviously poor listening in a small group discussing a controversial issue can lead to many problems that could be avoided if only the participant would listen.

The First Baptist Church in Newton, Massachusetts, conducted a series which focused on interpersonal communication. The activities they conducted with small groups would also be excellent preparation for a group concerned with controversial issues.

Session 1—Collages. Each group member used pictures and words from magazines and made a picture in which he tried to tell the group about himself. Various popular magazines were available for this.

Each group member was also asked to find one picture in a magazine that he felt best described himself. He was asked to put his name on the collage of himself and the descriptive picture and both were turned into the group leader.

Session 2—Collages Continued. Each person was asked to wear his descriptive picture. The collages were put up on the wall. Group members were asked to go around to the various collages and give descriptive words for each collage. When this was finished, each person was asked to identify his collage and tell his story about it.

Session 3—"Blind." In pairs, (each member selected a partner), participants took turns being "blind" and leading one another around anywhere, telling him what they saw, listening to him experience through other senses what he's "seeing."

The nonblindfolded person led the "blind" person around, telling him what he saw. The "blind" person told what he "saw" using other senses. After 10 minutes, the pair switched roles. When both had the experience of not seeing, the pair discussed their experience with each other for a few minutes, then the total group discussed feelings and meanings of the exercise.

The extent to which a group wants to participate in exercises such as outlined above will depend on the group. Some groups are much more ready to deal with issue discussions than others. But a prime requisite for good discussion is group members being open and knowing something about each other as persons.

Once the group members have some understanding of each other they are ready to get acquainted with the issue to be discussed. Depending on the issue, a group can be introduced to it in a variety of ways. A guest speaker can give a talk followed by questions, a film can be used, or the group can have a reading assignment before coming to the meeting. If the last technique is used, it's important that each member gets the reading assignment and has access to the material.

Once the participants have become acquainted with

each other and know something about the issue, they should be ready to discuss the problem areas—the questions that bother people and the points on which there is most apt to be disagreement. The discussion ought to come freely, leaving you as group leader with the role of a guide who helps the group remain focused on its subject.

But avoid leading them into the areas of personal concern until you feel they have progressed to the point of accepting each other as individuals. This will strengthen the likelihood that the group will discuss the issues without letting emotions carry them away. Facts about an issue also can help a group stay on an issue and keep emotions under control.

If it appears that the discussion is getting emotional and that tempers are about to flare, you can cool the situation by asking other members to help the antagonists analyze the basis of their disagreement. If worst came to worst, ask someone to respond to a question that may divert the discussion to another phase of the issue. Or you might suggest that perhaps the group has spent enough time on that particular aspect and propose another facet for discussion.

Occasionally it may be wise for a group to take a short break. Such a break can do much to change the tone of a discussion that may be moving in the direction of a personality clash. Remember, however, that this is an escapist solution; you may sacrifice a useful learning experience by not confronting the disagreement squarely and seeking its underlying reasons.

As a group leader, don't be afraid of leading discussion groups on controversial issues. These sessions can be exciting, and certainly important to the problems of people, and rewarding to you as group leader. Churches need men and women able to help a group look intelligently at the various aspects of an issue.

As adult groups tackle controversial issues, some of

them may reach a point where they achieve a consensus and feel moved to issue a declaration about their conclusions. A member of a discussion group that had met several times on an issue summarized his participation this way: "We discussed, even argued, but never got angry or personal. We found we like each other, anyway."

11

Selecting and Training Volunteers

The success of any religious adult education program depends on involvement, not only involvement of participants in various facets of the program, but involvement of volunteers to lead the small and large group discussions, teach the more formal classes, coordinate the more informal and less organized learning experiences, and to plan and administer the entire program.

"But nobody will volunteer," is the phrase often heard —and the excuse given why particular programs aren't offered.

So let's look at a program for recruiting and training adult education volunteers. As much as anything, working with volunteers is a matter of attitude on the part of professional staffs. There's got to be a feeling of optimism and confidence that volunteers can be obtained, that they're interested in training programs and self improvement, and that they can adequately plan and conduct the adult education program. Unless the professional staff has this attitude toward volunteerism, there can be no hope for success. The professional who says,

"Yes, but I can lead a small group discussion better than anyone else in the congregation," or "who else has the training that I've had—I'm the only one who can provide the accurate input that these people need—a volunteer who is ill-prepared may do more damage than good," will have problems getting volunteers.

This, I suppose, is part of the risk the professional staff must take. But the fact remains, if the adult education program is to expand and grow, members must be involved in the planning and carrying out of the program. And the professional staff must have confidence in the outcomes of the program—even though the programs may not be planned exactly as a professional may have planned them, and groups may not be led exactly the way the professional may have led them.

If we can agree then that volunteers are essential to a religious adult education program, the question is how do we get volunteers involved? There are several ways of thinking about recruiting and training volunteers. Let me suggest four stages in the process: (1) recruitment, (2) orientation, (3) continuing education, and (4) recognition.

RECRUITMENT

How to recruit volunteers is the question everyone wants answered with a formula or a pat "first-you-do-this-and-then-you-do-that" approach. "How do you get them to serve?" is the question heard around offices and coffee breaks in most organizations using volunteers, the church not excluded.

I have no formula answers, but some guidelines that should be helpful in recruitment.

Have a Job Description

Before anyone is recruited to any volunteer position the person doing the recruiting should have a specific job in mind for the volunteer. But how often do we hear someone say to a potential volunteer, "Say, John, how would you like to help us out with the adult education program at church?"

And John answers, "Doin' what?"

And he hears, "Oh, there's lots to do. We're trying to get some people lined up so we know what kinds of things we can do—then we'll know specifically."

That's what often happens. Yet to be effective in recruiting volunteers, someone or some group should have already decided what kind of adult education program is going to be offered and what specific kinds of volunteer assistance will be necessary.

Most volunteer positions fit into three broad categories:

1. Organizational leaders—those who assist in administering and coordinating adult education programs. Someone who may be responsible for coordinating all the small group discussion sessions that are operating in the church is an example.

2. Planning leaders—someone who serves on the adult education committee or some other planning group responsible for deciding about the nature and direction of the adult education programming.

3. Action leaders—those who lead small groups, teach classes, those responsible for carrying out the various phases of the adult education program.

So in a recruitment program, the recruiter must know in which of these three categories he needs volunteers and then must know specifically what volunteer position is open within that category. If the recruiter is looking for someone to lead a series of small group discussion sessions on drug abuse, then that information should be the basis for recruiting a volunteer.

Indicate a Time Commitment

Once a volunteer always a volunteer. That seems to be the tradition that has developed in the church. You're recruited to a task for life and you're embarrassed to leave the position. I think a more contemporary way to think about recruiting busy people for volunteer positions is to recruit them for a specific length of time. Serve one year on an adult education planning committee, serve two years as an adult education program coordinator, serve as discussion leader for five group discussion sessions. When the person has served the agreed upon time, then he should be free to leave or to re-volunteer for the same or some other task.

It's my feeling that people are much more likely to serve as a volunteeer if they know the amount of time they need to commit to the job.

Be Positive

"I know you're busy Mrs. Smith, but we really need help and the job won't take much of your time." But for Mrs. Smith to do a good job as a volunteer it will take time and probably lots of it. I think a much better approach is to say, "Look, Mrs. Smith, we'd like you to serve as a group discussion leader for a five-session course on understanding your teenager. This is an important area and it'll take some time in preparing for the meetings."

The positive approach will not only help the prospective volunteer know better what to expect of the position, but it will help give the position a feeling of importance. The volunteer knows that the sessions are important so he must allow time for preparing for them.

Don't apologize when you ask someone to serve. Indicate that the job is an important one, will take time, and is expected to be performed in a quality manner.

And emphasize with the potential volunteer that

there's much to be gained that will personally help the volunteer if he agrees to serve. Mention that the group leader, organizer or planner, always gains more from the experience than does the participant. The more effort put into a program, the more there's to be learned, and the hard working volunteer will be putting in much effort.

Training Program Available

Before a volunteer is recruited, he should know that there are training opportunities available for him so he will know how to do his job. And the recruiter should inform the potential volunteer that participating in the training program is a part of the responsibility that goes with the volunteer position.

We tend to be negative about training programs. "If you can make it you'll want to participate in the training program," or "Of course it isn't required, but we do have some training programs available for you." Again, I think we need to be positive. "We have some training programs available, and our volunteers are expected to attend."

Before I'm misunderstood, I'm not suggesting that all volunteers participate in the same training . . . no that's not what I'm suggesting. But no volunteer comes to his new job completely equipped to perform it. Participating in various training activities can help the volunteer do a better job and should be expected of him.

Direct and Indirect Recruitment

Some volunteers will recruit themselves. That is if an announcement is made in the church bulletin or elsewhere that volunteers are needed for various kinds of jobs, some people will come forward. But not very many. At least this has been my experience. Most have to be asked, personally and directly, before they'll serve as a volunteer.

So who asks them, who recruits volunteers for the church's adult education program? Several different types of people could: the professional staff, adult education committee members, and present volunteers are examples of three groups.

Recruiters, whoever they are, must be prepared for their task. They must know the nature of the position they're recruiting for well enough so they can look for the individual who can best fill the position, or the individual who comes closest to having the qualifications for the job. They must agree with the "positive approach" explained above, they must know the basic information about the church—size, kind of programs, they must know the total adult education program so they can tell prospective volunteers the relationship of the recruited position to the remainder of the program. They must be familiar with the training programs offered for new volunteers. And, like a salesman, they must be willing to accept a no answer and not be discouraged.

ORIENTATION PROGRAM

Once the volunteer has accepted, he must become acquainted with his job. And we must not forget that each volunteer brings to his new position unique abilities. Some things he'll be able to do well, and some things not at all.

To organize an orientation program, you must first determine the strengths and weaknesses of the volunteer. The more detailed the job description for the position, the easier it will be to determine areas where help is necessary.

At this point you may want to go back and look at the chapter "Learning as Content Acquisition." The nature of the learning experiences provided would be the same as those discussed in Chapter 8. Some of the training could be provided in groups where several volunteers have the same weakness, some of it must be provided on a one-to-one basis, and some of it the volunteer can get on his own if he's provided with appropriate material.

In organizing orientation experiences for new volunteers remember that this is one type of adult education. Much of what I have already discussed applies to volunteers as it applies to other adult learners.

CONTINUING LEARNING OPPORTUNITIES

Some of what the new volunteer considers an inadequacy will be competencies that do not need to be developed to a high level when the volunteer first starts. Thus, a long-range continuing education program is necessary. Again, a variety of learning experiences can be provided as explained earlier in the book.

Some of the continuing learning opportunities should focus on problems that the volunteer faces in his position. Re-reading the chapters on problem solving will be helpful at this point (Chapters 6 and 8).

The volunteer must feel that he's growing as he carries out his various volunteer duties. He too must feel that he's learning. Providing continuing learning opportunities can help assure that the volunteer's personal growth takes place. To help define further areas for continuing learning, the volunteer and the person who is in the position of supervising him should have an opportunity to meet and talk about the volunteer's work. Occasionally the volunteer feels he's competent in doing a particular task when in actuality he isn't. Discussions between the volunteer and his supervisor can help identify problem areas that the volunteer may not see by himself.

RECOGNITION

Recognition must not be forgotten as you work with volunteers. As we mentioned earlier, volunteers have needs too. One need is recognition.

There are several things that can be done. Often a simple "thank you" from the professional staff will accomplish as much as any other form of recognition. Other approaches to recognition are: (1) a recognition dinner for volunteers, (2) letters of appreciation written by the professional staff, and/or the adult education committee, (3) certificates for service—could be awarded at the recognition banquet, (4) names mentioned in bulletins, newspaper articles.

Recognition of volunteers is an easy thing to do . . . yet it can be overlooked. It must not be. It's important.

Notes

INTRODUCTION

1. Pierre Berton, *The Comfortable Pew* (Philadelphia: J. B. Lippincott Company, 1965), p. 108.

2. Elton Trueblood, "Introduction" in Wallace E. Fisher, *From Tradition to Mission* (New York: Abingdon Press, 1965), p. 7.

CHAPTER 1

1. Paul C. Johnson, "Illinois in Tradition," in *Proceedings of the Illinois State of Society Conference for Church Leaders* (Urbana, Illinois: Cooperative Extension Service, 1965).

2. William M. Ramsay, *Cycles and Renewal: Trends in Protestant Lay Education* (New York: Abingdon Press, 1969), p. 129.

CHAPTER 2

For Additional Reading

Fry, John R. *A Hard Look at Adult Christian Education.* Philadelphia: The Westminster Press, 1961.

Little, Lawrence C., ed. *The Future Course of Christian Adult Education.* Pittsburgh: The University of Pittsburgh Press, 1959.

Little, Lawrence C., ed. *Wider Horizons in Christian Adult Education.* Pittsburgh: The University of Pittsburgh Press, 1962.

CHAPTER 3

Some of this chapter appeared in Jerold W. Apps, "Understanding the Adult Learner," *The Lutheran Teacher*, XLIV (January, 1969), 20-21.

1. Cyril O. Houle, *The Inquiring Mind* (Madison, Wisconsin: The University of Wisconsin Press, 1961).

2. Robert J. Havighurst, *Developmental Tasks and Education* (New York: David McKay Company, 1961).

3. E. L. Thorndike, *Adult Learning* (New York: The Macmillan Company, 1928).

4. J. R. Kidd, *How Adults Learn* (New York: The Association Press, 1959), pp. 81-86.

5. Gary Dickinson, "Facts on Sight and Hearing in Training Adults," *Training in Business and Industry*, VI (October, 1969), 56-57.

6. Philip E. Slater, "Cultures in Collision," *Psychology Today*, IV (July, 1970), 31.

For Additional Reading

Burns, Hobert W., ed. *Sociological Backgrounds of Adult Education.* Boston: Center for the Study of Liberal Education for Adults, 1964.

Johnstone, John W. C., *et al. Volunteers for Learning.* Chicago: Aldine Publishing Company, 1965.

Kuhlen, Raymond G., ed. *Psychological Backgrounds of Adult Education.* Boston: Center for the Study of Liberal Education for Adults, 1963.

CHAPTER 4

1. John W. Gardner, *No Easy Victories* (New York: Harper Colophon Books, 1968) , p. 73.

For Additional Reading

Bergevin, Paul. *A Philosophy for Adult Education.* Philadelphia: The Westminster Press, 1959.

Ernsberger, D. J. *A Philosophy of Adult Christian Education.* Philadelphia: Westminster Press, 1959.

Gardner, John W. *No Easy Victories*. New York: Harper and Row, Publishers, 1968.

Rogers, Carl R. *Freedom to Learn*. Columbus, Ohio: Charles E. Merrill Publishing Company, 1969.

Snyder, Alton G. *Teaching Adults*. Valley Forge, Pennsylvania: The Judson Press, 1959.

CHAPTER 5

1. Developed by Professor Norman Alhisher, Management Consultant, University of Wisconsin Extension, Madison, Wisconsin, and member of Midvale Community Lutheran Church.

CHAPTER 6

For Additional Reading

Beckhard, Richard. *How to Plan and Conduct Workshops and Conferences*. New York: Association Press, 1956.

Bergevin, Paul E., and Dwight Morris. *Group Processes for Adult Education. Bloomington, Indiana:* Community Services in Adult Education, 1951.

Fansler, Thomas. *Discussion Methods for Adult Groups*. Washington, D.C.: American Association for Adult Education, 1934.

Fry, John R. *A Hard Look at Adult Christian Education*. Philadelphia: Westminster Press, 1961.

Hanson, Joseph J. *Our Church Plans for Adults*. Philadelphia: Judson Press, 1962.

Lowy, Louis. *Adult Education and Group Work*. New York: William Morrow and Company, 1955.

Luft, Joseph. *Group Processes*. Palo Alto, California: National Press, 1963.

Snyder, Alton G. *Teaching Adults*. Philadelphia: Judson Press, 1959.

Minor, Harold D. *Creative Procedures for Adult Groups*. Nashville, Tennessee: Abingdon Press, 1960.

Pamphlets of the Adult Education Association of the United States, Washington, D.C.:

No. 1, *How to Lead Discussions.* 1955.

No. 2, *Planning Better Programs.* 1955.

No. 4, *Understanding How Groups Work.* 1955.

No. 6, *How to Use Role Playing,* 1956.

No. 8, *Training Group Leaders.* 1956.

No. 9, *Conducting Workshops and Institutes.* 1956.

No. 14, *Better Boards and Committees.* 1957.

No. 15, *Streamlining Parliamentary Procedure.* 1957.

CHAPTER 9

1. Sara M. Steele, "Program Evaluation—A Broader Definition," *Journal of Extension,* VIII (Summer, 1970), 7.

2. *Ibid.*

CHAPTER 10

Some of this chapter appeared in Jerold W. Apps, "Disagreement Can Be Edifying," *Resource-Magazine of Parish Education,* XI (February, 1970), 10-13.

1. J. William Pfeiffer and John E. Jones, *A Handbook of Structured Experiences for Human Relations Training,* Vol. I (Iowa City, Iowa: University Associate Press, 1969), p. 34.

CHAPTER 11

1. Malcolm S. Knowles, *The Modern Practice of Adult Education* (New York: The Association Press, 1970), pp. 335-45.

5220